THE WAR
on
GOLD

Other books by Antony C. Sutton

Western Technology and Soviet Economic Development, 1917-1930

Western Technology and Soviet Economic Development, 1930-1945

Western Technology and Soviet Economic Development, 1945-1965

National Suicide: Military Aid to the Soviet Union

Wall Street and the Bolshevik Revolution

Wall Street and FDR

Wall Street and the Rise of Hitler

THE WAR

on

GOLD

ANTONY C. SUTTON

Seal Beach, California

Published by:

'76 Press
P.O. Box 2686
Seal Beach, Calif. 90740

International Standard Book Number 0-89245-008-8

Library of Congress Catalog Card Number 77-72297

Manufactured in the United States of America

Contents

Part Two: Gold Versus Paper

List of Tables and Charts

AUTHOR'S PREFACE

My sincere thanks to those who helped with ideas, enthusiasm and information.

In the United States: Bob Markle, my former editor, who suggested a book on gold; Jim Foley, a Pan American pilot who first told me about the barbaric relic; Jim Blanchard III who air mailed numerous packages of data on gold; and Charles van Niekerk for the translation of a speech by Paramount Chief Mantanzima.

In England: William Rees-Mogg, Editor of *The Times*, for an enlightening conversation.

In South Africa: former Secretary of Finance John E. Holloway; C. L. Stals, Managing Director of the South African Reserve Bank; F. R. "Red" Metrovich, Director of Valiant Press in Sandton City, for practical support; and Gail Crous of Cape Town for newspaper clippings.

Finally, '76 Press, and particularly Gary Allen and Wallis "Chip" Wood, who converted the manuscript to a book in short order with great efficiency.

To these, and others who helped along the way, thank you! Naturally all the arguments and errors are my own entirely.

November 1976

ANTONY C. SUTTON

GLOSSARY

Common words or phrases used by money manipulators, and their meanings in laymen's language.

Term as used by money manipulators:	Actual meaning, as used in this book:
A CRISIS IN CONFIDENCE	General public discovers it has been conned by politicians and bureaucrats.
RUN ON THE BANK	General public discovers it has been conned by the bankers.
WORTHLESS BARBARIC RELIC	Gold.
FEDERAL RESERVE NOTE	Rectangular piece of paper, about 2½" x 6", printed in green and black inks, inscribed "This note is legal tender for all debts, public and private." Private monopoly for such printed paper is held by the Federal Reserve System.
REAL MONEY	Paper fiat money issued by a state or private monopoly, or base metal coins (historically known as debased coinage).
LEGAL TENDER	Rectangular pieces of paper, about 2½" x 6", printed in green

	and black inks, inscribed "This note is legal tender for all debts, public and private."
SPECIAL DRAWING RIGHTS	International artificial or play money; has no physical attributes; comes into existence by official decree or whim as an entry on IBM cards.
GNOMES OF ZURICH	Zurich bankers, usually heavily invested in liquid assets including gold and silver. Reputation for privacy and protection of customers' accounts. (See also, RESPONSIBLE BANKING OFFICIALS)
RESPONSIBLE BANKING OFFICIALS	New York bankers, usually heavily invested in New York City bonds, REITs, Penn Central, Lockheed, W. T. Grant, and other "blue chip" equities. (Compare, GNOMES OF ZURICH)
SPECULATORS	Individuals who observe and act upon market signals. (Compare, TREASURY OFFICIALS)
TREASURY OFFICIALS	Government officials who observe and act upon market signals.
HOARDING	Precautionary saving of wealth (usually gold) by individuals. (See, RESERVES)
RESERVES (OF GOLD)	Precautionary saving of gold by Governments. (See, HOARDING)
MYSTIQUE	Individual confidence in gold as a store of wealth.
OFFICIAL ACTION IN GOLD MARKET	Gold sales by U.S. Treasury officials to depress price of gold.

	(See, Speculative Action in the Gold Market)
Speculative Action in the Gold Market	Gold purchases or sales by individuals anticipating gold prices moving higher or lower. (See, Official Action in Gold Market)
Speculation Against the Dollar	Foreign creditors presenting short-term claims for payment in gold. Usually associated with Gnomes of Zurich.

Terms on U.S. Treasury Blacklist (not to be used or referred to under any circumstances):

Assignat	Worthless French paper currency
Mandat	Worthless French paper currency
Continental Bill	Worthless American paper currency
Confederate Bills	Worthless American paper currency
Paper Pound of 1791-1820	Worthless British paper currency
Hungarian Pengo	Worthless Hungarian paper currency

CHAPTER ONE

Why Gold?

> *No State shall ... make any Thing but gold and silver Coin a Tender in Payment of Debts. ...*

The Constitution of the United States, Article One, Section 10.

IN MAY 1973 CORPORATE MONEY MANAGERS, Treasury and Government officials, academic theorists, and politicians around the world picked up their local newspapers to read that gold on the free London market had broken through the (then) almost incredible figure of $100 an ounce. By contrast, on the official market established by government decree, the price of gold was pegged at $42.22 an ounce, and the "professional" money managers in Washington considered even $42.22 "too high" for this residue of financial primitivism.

The professional money planners must indeed have felt uncomfortable. After all, for decades they had boldly averred in speeches and academic articles that gold was an unnecessary hangover — a "barbarous relic," according to Lord Keynes — from less sophisticated times. In this modern world of computers and business school techniques, we had no further need for gold in our "managed" economies. Or so they had argued.

Contemporary monetary columnists and pundits repeatedly stressed gold's gloomy future. Its role in world affairs, Sylvia Porter was certain, will be:

> *A minor one. And the role will become smaller, for gold is to be deliberately phased out of the monetary system over the years ahead, completing the process begun in Genoa in 1922.**

And here was gold busting exuberantly past $100 an ounce. It was a showing rarely matched by pork bellies or plywood futures.

Establishment journals and media reporting in the United States put the best face possible on a disturbing situation. *Business Week* reiterated that, Yes! gold was dead. But it admitted that obviously a lot of people around the world still had faith in gold and much less faith in paper money:

> *For several thousand years, the world has thought of gold as money. For several hundred years, it has lived increasingly on credit and still thought of gold as money. It will take some adjustment to think of paper money as the only money and gold as just like pork bellies.*†

As *Business Week* noted, gold has been thought of as money (usually as a store of value, less commonly for exchange purposes) almost since the dawn of civilization. Gold was used even before silver, although silver was more common, because native silver is rare and the metallurgical skills required to extract silver metal from complex ores came later than the discovery of simpler gold smelting techniques. While gold in early times was too scarce, and therefore too valuable, to use in day-to-day transactions, ancient civilizations in Egypt, China, Persia, and Babylon almost without exception left a record of their use of gold as a store of value. The historical evidence suggests that a paper money system can work for exchange purposes *only* if the option exists for conversion into gold. Never in history has an inconvertible paper system succeeded without a gold backing. But it is the store of value function of gold that is also

---

*San Francisco Chronicle, September 27, 1973.
†Business Week, May 19, 1973.

historically important; this function is unwisely ignored by modern economists and politicians.

Why gold has been accepted as money without question for several thousand years cannot be appreciated without looking at the unique role performed by gold as money and the alternatives to gold. Why has gold been universally accepted as money? Why have people distinguished between gold and almost all other commodities? Why is gold unique as a store of value and as a medium of exchange? We need first to look at history before we look further at today's war on gold.

We know that the Chinese used gold and silver from about 1200 B.C. onwards, Egypt from about 1000 B.C., Babylon and Minoa from at least the third century B.C. Byzantium achieved an extraordinary record — 800 years of monetary stability and prosperity with a gold coinage. Significantly, there was a remarkable uniformity of the standards of weight of gold coins used in these ancient empires. Widely separated localities over thousands of years in time had almost the same weight gold coins. We would perhaps expect coins to be portable, and large enough not to be lost in transit. But the uniformity was more precise than limits of overweight and underweight for transport purposes. This uniformity is a vital reflection of the intuitive and universal confidence that gold commands. In 1892 William Ridgeway listed the gold coin weight standards of these ancient empires as follows:*

TABLE 1-1: GOLD WEIGHT STANDARDS OF ANCIENT COINS

Gold Coin	Grains of gold per coin
Egyptian gold ring	127
Mycenaean	130-35
Homeric *talent* (or "ox unit")	130-35
Attic gold *stater*	135
Thasos	135
Rhodes	135
Cyzicus	130
Hebrew standard	130

*William Ridgeway, *The Origin of Coin and Weight Standards*, (Cambridge: 1892), p. 132.

Persian *daric*	130
Macedonian *stater*	130
Bactrian *stater*	130-32
Indian standard (7th century A.D.)	140
Phoenician gold unit (double)	260
Carthaginian	120
Sicily and Lower Italy	130-35
Etruscan unit	130-35
Gaulish unit	120
German	120

In brief, ancient gold coins were almost precisely uniform in weight: they ranged only between 120 grains for Carthaginian, German, and Gaulish coins to 135 grains for the Attic and Macedonian *staters*. The Homeric *talent* and the Persian *daric* were 130 grains; other ancient gold coins varied only between the limits of 120 and 140 grains. Why was there this remarkable uniformity over several thousand years, when communications were slow and cities widely separated? A. R. Burns suggests* that the constant weight originated at one trading center, either in Egypt or Chaldea, and emigrants and merchants carried coins to more distant parts where the weight was duplicated in other coins.

The important point is that these ancient gold coins were widely accepted in primitive times because of the *weight* of gold they were known to contain. It was the physical qualities of gold, the known content of gold of a particular fineness, the fact the coinage could not easily be expanded in supply or debased and counterfeited, the durability of gold, that made gold universally acceptable. Gold generated the all-important monetary prerequisite of *confidence*. Confidence that it would maintain its value. We shall see later that this psychological attribute of *confidence* is at the heart of the acceptibility of all money.

Even in ancient times, with primitive communications among vastly different peoples and customs, gold coins generated worldwide confidence; the requirement of confidence led to the adoption of similar coinage standards, and so similar units of

---

*A. R. Burns, *Money and Monetary Policy in Early Times*, (London: Kegan Paul, Trench Trubner & Co., Ltd., 1927), pp. 181-3.

weight evolved independently in different geographical areas. Full weight was essential for confidence and confidence was essential for coinage to circulate. Debasement by clipping or reducing the fineness was known but rarely adopted until medieval times. In fact debasement of the coinage could hardly exist in ancient communities not far removed from barter, which continued to barter and trade coins *by weight* concurrently after a monetary system was introduced.

In more modern societies, money is well integrated into the fabric of the economy, subject to political propaganda and decision-making, and so debasement and manipulation is difficult to isolate and recognize. Thus there exists a temptation for the state to depreciate its coinage for quick profit and to disguise the depreciation with a propaganda barrage.

Recognizing the essential requirement of confidence, ancient empires kept the value of their money constant for long periods without debasement. In the Persian Empire debasement occurred only in its declining years and even then took the form of a reduction in fineness to prevent export rather than political juggling with the metal content. In the Greek world, gold coins were almost always pure gold. Late in the Greek era the Greeks invented plated coins, but plated coins did not masquerade as genuine full weight and fineness gold coins. The Macedonian Empire maintained a pure coinage almost to the end. Only in the later Roman Empire did debasement constitute deliberate government policy. Gold coins of the Republic were almost always pure; after Augustus and the founding of the Roman Empire in 15 B.C., gold coins suffered progressive debasement under the strain of war and corrupt governments. It was not until the Roman Empire that the various techniques for coinage debasement were used widely on a large scale. The Eastern Empires of China, Persia, and Egypt were notable for their almost complete absence of debasement or devaluation until more modern times, with the exception of Chinese paper money which we shall describe below.

If in May 1973 Treasury officials and Establishment pundits had known more of monetary history and less of their grandiose plans for a new world order, they would not have been surprised when gold burst through $100 an ounce. Those immutable qualities that made gold acceptable in ancient times are still deeply embedded in the human psyche.

The Paper Money of Ancient China*

In many innovations the Chinese anticipated the Western world. Their abuse of paper fiat money is one such instance. The first European use of paper bank notes was recorded in Sweden in 1661.† By contrast, Marco Polo in his travels found the Chinese had used paper money in the thirteenth century. The Venetian traveler and explorer presents the following admiring account of the paper money system created by Kubla Khan.‡

HOW THE GREAT KAAN CAUSETH THE BARK OF TREES MADE INTO SOMETHING LIKE PAPER, TO PASS FOR MONEY OVER ALL HIS COUNTRY.

Now that I have told you in detail of the splendour of this City of the Emperor's, I shall proceed to tell you of the Mint which he hath in the same city, in the which he hath his money coined and struck, as I shall relate to you. And in doing so I shall make manifest to you how it is that the Great Lord may well be able to accomplish even much more than I have told you, or am going to tell you, in this Book. For, tell it how I might, you never would be satisfied that I was keeping within truth and reason!

The Emperor's Mint then is in this same City of Cambaluc, and the way it is wrought is such that you might say he hath the Secret of Alchemy in perfection, and you would be right! For he makes his money after this fashion.

He makes them take of the bark of a certain tree, in fact of the Mulberry Tree, the leaves of which are the

---

*The key source for this section is a treatise by the Chinese scholar Ma-twan-lin, "The Examination on Currency," contained in Volumes VIII and IX of his Great Encyclopaedia. There is an English language summary, W. Vissering, On Chinese Currency: Coin and Paper Money, (Leiden: E. J. Brill, 1877), reprinted in 1968 by Ch'eng-wen Publishing Company, Taiwan.

†The first regular issue. There was an emergency paper issue in 1574: the Leyden Taler, formed as a round coin from pages of prayer books when Leyden was under seige by the Spanish.

‡Original from Henry Yule's edition of Marco Polo's travels, reprinted in W. Vissering, op. cit., pp. 26-8.

food of the silkworms, — these trees being so numerous that whole districts are full of them. What they take is a certain fine white bast or skin which lies between the wood of the tree and the thick outer bark, and this they make into something resembling sheets of paper, but black. When these sheets have been prepared they are cut up into pieces of different sizes. The smallest of these sizes is worth a half tornesel; the next, a little larger, one tornesel; one a little larger still, is worth half a silver groat of Venice; another a whole groat; others yet two groats, five groats, and ten groats. There is also a kind worth one Bezant of gold, and others of three Bezants, and so up to ten.

All these pieces of paper are issued with as much solemnity and authority as if they were of pure gold or silver; and on every piece a variety of officials, whose duty it is, have to write their names, and to put their seals. And when all is prepared duly, the chief officer deputed by the Kaan smears the Seal entrusted to him with vermilion, and impresses it on the paper, so that the form of the Seal remains stamped upon it in red: the Money is then authentic. Any one forging it would be punished with death. And the Kaan causes every year to be made such a vast quantity of this money, which costs him nothing, that it must equal in amount all the treasures in the world.

With these pieces of paper, made as I have described, he causes all payments on his own account to be made, and he makes them to pass current universally over all his Kingdoms and provinces and territories, and whithsoever his power and sovereignty extends. And nobody, however important he may think himself, dares to refuse them on pain of death. And indeed everybody takes them readily, for wheresoever a person may go throughout the Great Kaan's dominions he shall find these pieces of paper current, and shall be able to transact all sales and purchases of goods by means of them just as well as if they were coins of pure gold. And all the while they are so light that ten bezants' worth does not weight one golden Bezant.

Furthermore all merchants arriving from India or other countries, and bringing with them gold or silver or gems and pearls, are prohibited from selling to any one but the Emperor. He has twelve experts chosen for this business, men of shrewdness and experience in such affairs; these appraise the articles, and the Emperor then pays a liberal price for them in those pieces of paper. The merchants accept his price readily, for in the first place they would not get so good a one from anybody else, and secondly they are paid without any delay. And with this papermoney they can buy what they like anywhere over the Empire, whilst it is also vastly lighter to carry about on their journeys. And it is a truth that the merchants will several times in the year bring wares to the amount of 400,000 bezants, and the Grand Sire pays for all in that paper. So he buys such a quantity of those precious things every year that his treasure is endless, whilst all the time the money he pays away costs him nothing at all. Moreover several times in the year proclamation is made through the city that any one who may have gold or silver or gems or pearls, by taking them to the Mint shall get a handsome price for them. And the owners are glad to do this, because they would find no other purchaser give so large a price. Thus the quantity they bring in is marvellous, though those who do not choose to do so may let it alone. Still, in this way, nearly all the valuables in the country come into the Kaan's possession.

When any of those pieces of paper are spoilt — not that they are so very flimsy neither — the owner carries them to the Mint, and by paying 3 per cent on the value he gets new pieces in exchange. And if any Baron, or any one else soever, hath need of gold or silver or gems or pearls, in order to make plate, or girdles or the like, he goes to the Mint and buys as much as he list, paying in this papermoney.

Now, you have heard the ways and means whereby the Great Kaan may have, and in fact has, more treasure than all the Kings in the World; and you know all about it and the reason why.

The Chinese ultimately found by bitter experience that Marco Polo's admiration of their mulberry-bark paper money was not well founded. History suggests that for money to perform its functions, it has to retain an intrinsic value corresponding to its nominal value. The Khan's advisers carefully warned the Emperor that mulberry bark paper money was intrinsicly worthless and needed specie backing in order for people to have confidence in its value. At first the Chinese mulberry bark paper notes were backed by gold, silver, copper and iron equal to 3/7ths of the outstanding notes. In China copper and iron performed the functions of supplying the required intrinsic value rather than scarce gold and silver. In fact the origin of Chinese paper money grew out of a problem rarely found elsewhere in world monetary history: iron and copper specie, especially the heavy iron money of Western China, were too troublesome to pass from hand to hand. So paper money originated as paper bills or receipts for specie passed between private persons. The State recognized the private profit, intervened in the transactions, and made paper money a State monopoly.

About 1000 A.D. the state-issued paper money became legal tender, and was readily accepted as long as it remained convertible into specie (iron, copper, gold, and silver). The first series of government notes remained convertible for 65 years or so; then the government limited conversion to a single opportunity every three years. In practice, at the end of each three-year term few bills were presented for conversion. "The consequence was the government became improvident, and the increasing wants of the Army induced it at last to use the reserve fund deposited in the bank."* After another century the "number of circulating bills was certainly twenty times as much [as first issue] and consequently their value was injured the more."†

A Chinese author described the money bills of the Mongol dynasty in this fashion:

> *Already were the bills in consequence of the over-issue no more fit to measure the value of all merchandise, and when in consequence of the confusions of war*

---

*W. Vissering, *op. cit.*, p. 172.
†*Ibid.*, p. 174.

there was for the government expenditure no sufficient quantity of money to meet the want, continually new bills were printed, the result was that the bills had no value while commodities fetched high prices, and when at last they were not accepted any more, that law by which they had been instituted, was repealed. At the time that they had their full value, the bills were generally used as balancing money but in the times of their decay when the deposit which should have backed them was not sufficient, more paper money was constantly made, till at last they [the bills] were not current any more.

The inflation of the Vietnamese War, followed by suspension of dollar convertibility in 1971, parallels the Chinese situation of 700 years ago. The Chinese wars with the Tartars brought about a vast increase in the money supply, and,

*Eager as they had been before to keep the notes in their possession, they were now anxious to redeem them, but though presenting them at the fixed interval no specie payment was obtained. The holders of these already considerably depreciated bills of exchange received instead of money a new sort of notes called credit notes.**

The Chinese government decreed that paper money was to be accepted without question as equivalent to "hard" money:

It was ordered by law that what in the future should be stipulated for in iron and copper money, should be paid partly in bills, these would have a value corresponding to that of metallic Money.†

Ultimately the oppressive Mongol paper money system was a major factor in their expulsion from China. It was not until the nineteenth century and penetration of Western ideas and practices that the Chinese again adopted paper currency. After World War II, that fiat money was used to generate one of the worst inflations on record.

---

*Ibid.
†Ibid., p. 15.

The Gold Solidus of the Byzantine Empire

By contrast to the Chinese paper system, the "Bezant" mentioned in Marco Polo's description of Kubla Khan's Empire was a gold coin minted in the Byzantine Empire and which represented the most extraordinarily successful use of the gold standard in history. The 1,000-year history of Byzantine gold coins, minted from 491 A.D. to 1453 A.D., began long before the Chinese discovered paper money and lasted long after the collapse of Kubla Khan's mulberry bark receipts.

From 491 A.D. to 1000 A.D., the solidus, or bezant, was coined with a fineness of .95, as are many of today's gold coins. (This is a greater fineness than the .85 "coin melt" bars found in Fort Knox today.*) After the collapse of the Roman Empire the Byzantine Empire dominated trade from the Atlantic Ocean to China; under Constantine the gold solidus became the standard for the next 800 years and the basis of a vast trading empire stretching throughout the known world.

The quality of Byzantine coinage was such that it was accepted freely, without question, from China to Brittany, from the Baltic Sea to Ethiopia. Bezants were used, not only by Byzantine travelers and merchants, but by those of other countries as well. Even medieval England's Exchequer rolls were kept in bezants. Not until Alexium in the twelfth century did the Byzantine Empire fall.

In summary, the first two-thousand years of coinage — up to the end of the Byzantine Empire — suggest the crucial role of gold in a monetary system. Gold coins circulated by weight with other metallic coins and barter. Barter inhibited debasement of gold coins, because it offered alternative media of exchange. In the Byzantine bezant of constant purity and fineness we can identify the first worldwide gold standard. Inflation in the form of reducing the monetary standard and speeding up the primitive coinage process was known. Debasement (that is, reducing the weight or purity of gold coins) was also known, and plated gold coins were used as early as the fifth century B.C. A. R. Burns comments as follows on such plated coins:

---

*Or presumed to be in Fort Knox. There is skepticism about the existence of a U.S. gold stock which has not been physically audited in decades. See p. 114 for fineness of reserves.

They are of interest because they offer the nearest approach in the ancient world to modern paper money: they were a currency of which the metallic value was much less than the legal value, and they offered far more scope for inflation without resort to recoinage than debasement or devaluation.*

From this early historical experience we observe that states always held the power of coinage close to the seat of political power and that war, corruption, or just plain greed led to debasement and inflation of the money supply. Only a system with full weight coins offers protection against expansion of state political power through the monetary system. In brief, the power to coin money is intimately related to the acquisition of political power. Thus it has always been, and thus it is today.

---

*A. R. Burns, *op. cit.*, p. 464.

PART ONE

THE HISTORICAL EXPERIENCE

CHAPTER TWO

Not Worth a Continental

> *Our American Bankers have found that for which the ancient alchymists [sic] sought in vain; they have found that which turns everything into gold in their own pockets, and it is difficult to persuade them that a system which is so very beneficial to themselves, can be very injurious to the rest of the community.*
>
> William Gouge, *A Short History of Banking and Paper Money in the United States*, (Philadelphia: T. W. Ustick, 1833)

AT THE END OF THE EIGHTEENTH CENTURY, and in the first few years of the nineteenth, three contemporary powers, France, England, and the emerging United States, suffered through bitter experiences with paper fiat money systems. These experiences were sufficiently unpleasant, and indeed tragic in many aspects, that for a century thereafter, until the outbreak of war in Europe in 1914, the civilized world operated on a full gold standard with only occasional and temporary lapses into paper money schemes. In general the nineteenth century witnessed an intellectual environment fully aware of the virtues of a stable gold standard and the vices of paper money.

These three monetary episodes, now virtually unknown in the United States, are: (a) the French assignat-mandat inflation of 1789 to 1796. The conclusion of this experiment in inflation was the public burning in the Place Vendôme of all paper money. The subsequent introduction of the gold Napoleon began a period when gold had a major psychological impact on the French nation, even down to present-day French attitudes to gold.

Then came: (b) the British paper pound of 1797-1821. This experiment came just after the cross-channel French assignat-mandat inflationary chaos. Because of the proximity and awareness of the French monetary disaster, England backed off the paper pound and by 1821 restored full specie convertibility. Gold convertibility was retained until 1914, but probably because the miserable effects of a paper currency that were fully felt in France were dampened in England, the lesson of gold penetrated less deeply into the British psyche.

Our third example is: (c) the American Continental Bill of 1775 to 1779. The lessons of the Continental currency were incorporated into the U.S. Constitution but barely penetrated American consciousness. The error of the Continental was subsequently repeated with the Civil War Greenback and naively incorporated into the note-issuing authority of the Federal Reserve Act of 1913. The Continental and the Greenback experiences had little lasting impact in the United States, beyond the legacy of the classic description "Not worth a Continental," and a now-disputed Article 1, Section 10 in the U.S. Constitution.

The French Assignat of 1789 to 1796

The arguments of the eighteenth-century French inflationists bear a striking similarity to the arguments of the "soft money" school in the Greenback era of the 1860s and the "let's demonetize gold" era of the 1970s.

In 1789 slow trade and economic difficulties in France brought forth conflicting appeals to introduce paper money on the one hand and reminders of earlier cataclysmic experiences with John Law's paper money between 1716 and 1720 on the other. After much prompting, the French National Assembly recommended a "limited" issue of four hundred million paper livres. Under pressure of immediate economic necessity John Law and his legacy were brushed aside by the majority of the National Assembly, much as our modern inflationists have brushed aside the history of paper money. The first assignats were based upon the security of seized Church property and were circulated amidst government pronouncements that prosperity would once again be brought to France and that in the near future paper assignats would prove to be more valuable than gold coins.

For a while everything went well. Credit and trade revived. Prosperity once again spread across France. But after six months the government found it had spent the authorized four hundred million assignats, and:

> *The condition of opinion in the Assembly was, therefore, chaotic; a few schemers and dreamers were loud and outspoken for paper money; many of the more shallow and easy-going were inclined to yield; and more thoughtful endeavoured to breast the current.* *

Montesquieu's report of August 1790 recommended, albeit with some reluctance, another issue of paper assignats. In spite of the dangers of price inflation, he said, "We must save the country and the increased money supply would revive France."

Just as today's paper-money proponents suggest that "times are different" from 1790, so did Montesquieu argue that France in 1790 was different from the France of John Law in 1716. Paper assignats, it was asserted, were guaranteed by national lands and the good faith and good sense of the French people. Chabroud argued the merits of paper money as follows:

> *The earth is the source of value; you cannot distribute the earth in a circulating value, but this paper becomes representative of that value and it is evident that the creditors of the nation will not be injured by taking it.* †

Today it is argued in a similar vein that Federal Reserve notes and credit are backed by all of American wealth and technology, and that in any event "we owe it to ourselves." Unfortunately, neither Chabroud nor his modern counterparts discuss the vital question that paper only represents wealth as long as recipients of paper money have confidence of a lasting valid claim on wealth, which they can pass on to others in exchange or hold as a reliable

---

*Andrew Dickson White, *Fiat Money Inflation in France*, (Toronto, Canada: Privately published, 1914), p. 36.
†*Ibid.*, p. 41.

store of value. Statesman Talleyrand presented the most incisive anti-paper money case to the French people:

> *You can, indeed, arrange it so that people shall be forced to take a thousand livres in paper for a thousand livres in specie, but you can never arrange it so that a man shall be obliged to give a thousand livres in specie for a thousand livres in paper — in that fact is embedded the entire question; and on account of that fact the whole system fails.* *

Talleyrand was saying, in other words, that there is no guarantee men will always surrender gold for paper; they are far more likely just to surrender paper and hoard gold, or, as Gresham's Law† puts it, "Bad money drives out good."

This eighteenth-century French debate involved almost all newspapers of the day and most eminent academics. Reminders that John Law's paper issues had brought ruin to France, and only a few decades earlier at that, were in vain. On September 29, 1790, another 800 million assignats were authorized by the National Assembly. France was now set upon an irreversible inflationary course. Specie disappeared from circulation. Small silver and copper coins became scarce and replaced by a myriad of different paper notes. Church bells were melted down, and churches were required to send surplus church utensils to the melting pot. Citizens were exhorted to send in their plate and jewelry for melting. Even the King reportedly sent gold and silverplate for conversion into small change coins.

Prices escalated, and the demand for both paper currency and small coins escalated in proportion. By 1791, under these immediate pressures, the previous pledges to restrict the printing of assignats were forgotten; another 600 million were run off the printing presses. This issue spurred yet another round of price increases and subsequent depression. Uncertain of the future value of money, investment declined. The race was on to acquire hard goods, almost any goods, to preserve assets. Speculation in goods replaced thrift and enterprise.

Ibid., p. 43.
†See p. 121.

This economic stress led to civil disturbances. In February 1791, mobs stormed the Paris food shops. In response the State terrorized shopkeepers and merchants, blaming them for the rising prices created by the Government itself when it expanded the money supply. Extraordinary taxes were imposed. Trade collapsed. The rich, prosperous, and intelligent fled France. The less prosperous and the non-producers were left to face the inevitable collapse of the French economy.

Then, as today, the Government thought of price controls and imposed the ultimate economic absurdity — the so-called Law of the Maximum. Committees of expert economists were appointed to fix prices, and these maximum prices were placed on all goods. Consequently, no food came into the cities for trade. The threat of the guillotine, even the daily lists of farmers and merchants executed for non-compliance with the Law of the Maximum, did little to encourage trade in Paris and other cities. So the French State decreed that any person selling gold or silver coins, or making any difference in a transaction between paper and specie, was to be "imprisoned in irons for six years, that anyone who refused to accept a payment in assignats, or accepted assignats at a discount should pay a fine of three thousand francs."*

A second offense was punishable with 20 years imprisonment in irons; by May 1794, any person who asked before a transaction in what medium payment was to be made (that is, paper or gold) was subject to the death penalty. This terror reached its apogee on November 13, 1793, when in a final gasp, the State banned all trading in and use of precious metals. After two more years of economic chaos, at December 1795 fifty thousand million paper assignats were in circulation and their purchasing power was almost zero. A gold franc might be exchanged for 600 paper francs — if an exchange could be made.

Then came the day when even the politicians in the National Assembly and the bureaucrats saw the light of dawn. The French burned all of their paper money and the means of its production. As described by Andrew Dickson White:

> . . . on *February 18, 1796, at nine o'clock in the*

---

*Ibid., p. 79.

*morning, in the presence of a great crowd, the machin-
ery, plates, and paper for printing assignats were
brought to the Place Vendôme and there, on the spot
where the Napoleon Column now stands, these were
solemnly broken and burned.**

One final issue of paper money made in 1796, the mandats, promptly dropped to a mere three percent of face value within several months. So France turned to the gold Napoleon and for a century thereafter prospered on a full gold standard. Today French private citizens, in response to this deeply respected monetary lesson, own two or three times more gold than the French Government, which itself has a healthy respect and acquisitive instinct for gold. This suggests the lessons of the assignat and the mandat were not lost. French citizens and most French politicians today have no illusions that paper is as good as gold.

While the French assignat-mandat systems were brought about by "hard times," the British "paper pound" experiment of 1797-1821 was brought about by a war, much as the final steps to the American "going off gold" campaign in 1971 were brought about by the burdens of the Vietnamese War.

The British Paper Pound (1797-1821)

Our second eighteenth century example of a paper money fiasco comes from just across the English channel. In 1793, when Britain went to war with France, the British pound was a sound money medium fully convertible into gold. Gold was exchanged at the rate of 123¼ grains of 22-carat gold to the pound sterling. Silver coins were legal tender by tale (count) under £ 25 and by weight above £ 25. Legal tender paper money did not exist, although approximately   12 million of Bank of England notes circulated in the London area and perhaps the same amount of "country bank" notes circulated outside London. About £ 20 to £ 30 million in gold coins were also in circulation; these were known as "Guineas," after the source of their gold metal.

The financial mini-panic of 1792, prompted by anticipation of war with France, was quieted by a Government loan of £ 2 million to failing businesses. War expenditures increased only

---

*Ibid, p. 92.

slowly at first, more rapidly later, while the Government relied on the Bank of England for loans to cover its deficits. By 1796 gold bullion in the Bank vaults was down to £ 400,000 (from £ 7 million in 1794) and its outstanding liabilities had increased to almost £ 16 million. The alarming bullion drain prompted the Bank of England directors to visit Prime Minister Pitt. Subsequently, at a meeting of the English establishment (the King, Prime Minister Pitt, the Lord Chancellor, the Duke of Portland, and the Earl of Liverpool), it was agreed to ask the Bank of England to stop gold payments "until the sense of Parliament can be taken." Thereupon a not-too-unhappy Bank of England showed this State order to its customers (without explaining the behind-the-scenes political action), and declined to exchange gold for notes. Thus, convertibility was in effect suspended for the Bank of England, but not for other note-issuing banks. The House of Lords debate which followed suspension generated numerous statements that the inconvertible paper pound would depreciate, slowly and inevitably, and unless made convertible into gold, the pound sterling would go the way of the French assignat.

The importance of convertibility in this and other banking panics is emphasized in a contemporary commentary by a Scots banker:*

> *On Monday the 20th, they came to our counting house in considerable numbers, evidently under the impression of terror, calling for payment of their notes that had been lodged at interest. This lasted the whole of that week and the two first days of the following. Nor was it confined to us alone, for the public banks experienced it in a still greater degree, and we were beginning to think there was to be a similar, perhaps a still severer, demand on us than what had taken place in 1793; when, early in the morning of Wednesday, the 1st March, an express arrived from London to the directors of the Bank of Scotland from Thomas Coutts & Co., their correspondents there, informing them that the demand for gold on the Bank of England had risen to such*

---

*William Forbes, *The Memoirs of a Banking House*, (Edinburgh: Privately published, 1859).

an alarming height that the Directors had thought it proper to state the circumstance to the Chancellor of the Exchequer, who immediately procured an order of the Privy Council to be issued, prohibiting that bank from making any more issues of specie in exchange for their notes.

Mr. Mansfield, who was a director of the Bank of Scotland, informed our Mr. Anderson of this interesting event, and he immediately brought the intelligence to me, a little before the usual hour of commencing business. My ideas, at various times during the course of the war, had been often not a little gloomy when I thought of the state of things in the kingdom, and indeed in Europe; but now it was that I certainly did think the nation was ruined beyond redemption, when so novel and alarming a circumstance had taken place at the Bank of England, which had ever been considered as the bulwark of public and private credit.

Mr. Hay, Mr. Anderson, my son and I all repaired as fast as possible to the counting-house, which at ten o'clock was crowded as usual with people demanding gold. We were soon joined by Mr. Simpson, cashier, and Mr. James, deputy-governor of the Royal Bank, and by Mr. Fraser, the treasurer of the Bank of Scotland, and we sent for Mr. Hog, manager of the British Linen Company, for all ceremony or etiquette of public or private banks was now out of the question, when it had become necessary to think of what was to be done for our joint preservation on such an emergency.

Thence we repaired to the Bank of Scotland, where their directors were assembled, and after some time spent in consultation with them, it was agreed that there was no choice left but to follow the Bank of England, and suspend all further payments in specie. The Lord Provost instantly gave orders for calling a meeting of the principal inhabitants that day at two o'clock, which was very numerously attended considering the shortness of the notice . . . .

Strictly as a matter of law the Scots note-issuing banks, unlike the Bank of England, could not hide behind the Privy Council order suspending payment in specie; the Scots banks were required to pay in specie or default. But more to the point, the way in which a run on a bank develops and the critical importance of *confidence* — the assumption by noteholders that all is well — is brought out by banker William Forbes as he continues his story:

> *. . . After stating the order of Council for suspending the payments in specie by the Bank of England, the similar resolution was instantly and unanimously entered into by those present to give every countenance and support to the Edinburgh banks — including our firm — by receiving their notes in payment with the same readiness as heretofore, and a handbill was instantly circulated over Edinburgh, and inserted in all the newspapers. Expresses were likewise dispatched to Glasgow, Greenock, Paisley, Ayr, Perth, Dundee and Aberdeen — at all which places there were banks — to inform them of what was passing.*
>
> *The instant this resolution of paying no more specie was known in the street, a scene of confusion and uproar took place of which it is utterly impossible for those who did not witness it to form an idea. Our counting-house, and indeed the offices of all the banks, were instantly crowded to the door with people clamorously demanding payment in gold of their interest-receipts, and vociferating for silver in change of our circulating paper. It was in vain that we urged the order of Council — which, however, applied, merely to the Bank of England — and the general resolution adopted by all other banks in Edinburgh. They were deaf to every argument and although no symptom, nor indeed threatening of violence appeared, their noise, and the bustle they made, was intolerable; which may be readily believed when it is considered that they were mostly of the lowest and most ignorant classes, such as fish-women, carmen, street porters and butcher's men, all bawling out at once for change, and jostling one another in their endeavours who should get nearest to the table, behind which were*

cashiers and ourselves endeavouring to pacify them as
well as we could.

Of our interest-receipts we were prompt in payment; but instead of giving our own circulating notes, as
heretofore, we paid the value in notes of the public
banks . . . the sums had been deposited with us not in
specie, but in such notes as we now gave back to the
holders. With regard to our circulating notes . . . we felt
the hardship on the holders, who were deprived of the
means of purchasing with ready money the necessaries
of life, as there were no notes of less value than twenty
shillings and it was with the utmost difficulty they could
get change anywhere else; for the instant it was known
that payments in specie were suspended, not a person
would part with a single shilling that they could keep,
and the consequence was that both gold and silver specie was hoarded up and instantly disappeared . . . .

Saturday was the day on which we had the sever-
est outcry to encounter . . . many master-tradesmen requested in the most earnest manner to have a little silver
for enabling them to pay their workpeople. All we could
do when sensible that their demand proceeded from real
necessity, was privately to change a note or two by taking them into a separate room, for we durst not do it
openly in the counting-house for fear of raising a riot.

It was a matter of agreeable surprise to see in how
short a time after the suspension of paying in specie, the
run on us ceased. . . . It was remarkable, also after the
first surprise and alarm was over, how quietly the
country submitted as they still do, to transact all
business by means of bank notes for which the issuers
give no specie as formerly. The wonder was the greater
because the act of the Privy Council first, and after-
wards the act of Parliament, applied merely, as I have already said, to the Bank of England, while all other
banks, both in England and Scotland, were left to carry
on their business without any protection from Parliament.

Parliament confirmed suspension of convertibility with the

Bank Restriction Act of 1797, which was extended annually for another 25 years. Notes were not made legal tender but they were authorized for Bank of England issue. Other banks, not allowed to issue notes, when presented with demands from customers exchanged their own notes for Bank of England notes. Gold and silver promptly went into hoarding and Britain went onto a paper-money standard.

Fortunately, the Government of the day was sufficiently competent to restrict expenditures even in time of war and the French assignat crisis almost guaranteed cautious use of the right of notes issue. Nevertheless, a steady increase in notes circulating and a budget deficit brought two inevitable consequences: (a) a rise in prices, and (b) an increase in the price of gold bullion.

By 1809 one pound sterling was worth only 107 instead of 123¼ grains of gold. In 1810 Parliament appointed the Bullion Committee to investigate the "high" price of bullion, which was more accurately the *low* value of the pound. The Bullion Report of 1810 contained forthright conclusions, including the observation that when a "paper currency originally founded on and convertible into coin has become inconvertible, it can only be kept up to its proper value by a limitation of its quantity based on observation of the price of bullion and the foreign exchanges."*

The Bullion Report of 1810 is a major historical investigative document whose arguments and conclusions still have relevence in the late twentieth century. Members of the Parliamentary Committee which heard evidence and wrote the Report included banker Alexander Baring and financial writer Henry Thornton.† An anonymous and well-informed Continental witness, usually conjectured to be N. M. Rothschild, provided the Committee with a wealth of personal experience on the behaviour of money markets.

---

*Edwin Cannan, *The Paper Pound*, (London: P. S. King & Son, 1919) p. XXii. This book includes a reprint of the Bullion Committee Report.

†Henry Thornton (1760-1815), banker and economist, was a notable, but today overlooked, monetary theorist with one major work: *An Enquiry into the Nature and Effects of the Paper Credit of Great Britain (1802)*, (New York: Farrar & Rinehart, 1939), with introduction by F. A. v. Hayek. Thornton is better known as a religious writer and a prominent member of the evangelist Clapham Sect. In *An Enquiry* Thornton makes a methodical and rigorous examination of the effects of an increase in currency; it is an analysis that could, with profit, be read at the U.S. Treasury in the 1970s.

Section I of the Report presented evidence on the "high price of gold." Most witnesses pointed to the fact that there had been no rise in the price of gold on the Continent, nor any shortage of gold in England, but that since 1797 there had been an excess of bank notes "not convertible at will into coin which is exportable." Hence the ratio of gold to bank notes changed; that is, it required more paper pounds to acquire the same amount of gold. The Bullion Report included a statement summerizing this historical experience:

> *The Committee cannot refrain from expressing it to be their opinion after a very deliberate consideration of this part of the subject, that it is a great practical error to suppose that the Exchanges with Foreign Countries, and the price of Bullion, are not liable to be affected by the amount of a paper currency, which is issued without the condition of payment in specie at the will of the holder. That the Exchanges will be lowered, and the price of Bullion raised, by an issue of such paper to excess, is not only established as a principle by the most eminent authorities upon Commerce and Finance; but its practical truth has been illustrated by the history of almost every State in modern times which has used a paper currency; and in all those countries, this principle has finally been resorted to by their Statesmen as the best criterion to judge by, whether such currency was or was not excessive.* *

In other words, the supply of gold is relatively fixed and the supply of paper money is relatively easily expanded, so if a State issues more bank notes the price of gold will rise.

In Section III, the Committee reported on "Control of the Note Issue." While exculpating the Bank of England for following its normal routine after suspension of convertibility, the Report pointed out that the "Suspension of convertibility took away the check caused by a drain of gold and left the paper currency without sufficient limitation." The situation was exacerbated by the "usury law" which fixed maximum rates of interest, and so prevented market forces from correcting the excesses.

---

*Bullion Report, *op. cit.*, p. 36.

After a critical swipe at the Bank of England directors who "see the truth so little that they actually claim that their principle could work equally effectually with a much lower rate of discount," the Bullion Committee concluded that the note issue had been large, was still increasing, and that the only guard against excess is convertibility into gold, while the only proper reform would be resumption of cash payments for gold. The Committee recommended convertibility within two years. A summary of the Committee's conclusions contained the following:

> *Opinion, which they submit to the House: That there is at present an excess in the paper circulation of this Country, of which the most unequivocal symptom is the very high price of Bullion, and next to that, the low state of the Continental Exchanges: that this excess is to be ascribed to the want of a sufficient check and control in the issues of paper from the Bank of England; and originally, to the suspension of cash payments, which removed the natural and true control. For upon a general view of the subject, Your Committee are of opinion that no safe, certain, and constantly adequate provision against an excess of paper currency, either occasional or permanent, can be found, except in the convertibility of all such paper into specie. Your Committee cannot, therefore, but see reason to regret that the suspension of cash payments, which, in the most favourable light in which it can be viewed, was only a temporary measure, has been continued so long; and particularly, that by the manner in which the present continuing Act is framed, the character should have been given to it of a permanent war measure.**

The clarity of the Bullion Report is refreshing: *Inflation is an increase in the money supply.* It has occasionally been an increase in the supply of gold, but usually is an increase in the issue of paper notes. This inflation is translated into higher prices. Only convertibility of paper money into specie, limited in supply, provides adequate protection against inflation.

**Ibid.*, p. 66.

The Report contained none of the present-day weasel words, algebraic manipulations, finger-pointing at trade unions or businessmen, cries about conspicuous consumption or other handy, but entirely innocent, targets. The Bullion Report of 1810 laid it out clearly and simply: Inflation is an increase in the money supply. To restrict inflation you look to the note-issuing authority, whether it is a central bank or a Government mint, and restrict the note issue. The only effective restriction of a note issue, in the light of experience, is convertibility into specie, such as gold and silver.

Our first two examples of the paper versus gold controversy have been taken from Europe. The United States has had its own bitter experiences with inflationary paper money. So we next turn to the story of the Continental Bill.

The Continental Currency Fiasco

Early American settlers used gold and silver, and occasionally commodities such as tobacco and corn, as their medium of exchange. In 1690 the first North American fiat money was issued in Massachusetts, to enable the Government to pay its soldiers for several military expeditions. As the quantity of this paper issued increased, so its value in gold and silver decreased.*

Other colonies imitated the Massachusetts paper issues with similar results. Of these issues Pennsylvania had a reputation for moderation (recorded by Adam Smith) but even Pennsylvania paper sank in value below gold and silver. William Gouge presents evidence that "the paper was never at a less discount than eleven percent if gold be taken as the standard, or seven percent if silver be the standard."†

This Colonial Government scrip fluctuated in value depending on the credit of the issuing Government and the amount printed. Although much inferior in quality and acceptability to

---

*William M. Gouge, *A Short History of Paper Money and Banking in the United States*, (Philadelphia: T. W. Ustick, 1833). Gouge was the designer and administrator of the Independent Treasury System which handled central monetary functions until the establishment of the Federal Reserve System in 1914. See Plate 7, Part II of Gouge for tabular statement of relative values.

†*Ibid.*, p. 9, Part II.

Bank paper, Gouge points out that "Its character was better understood by the people. They knew the authority of the Government, and the resources of the Government. When they were injured, they knew by whom they were injured, if not to what extent."*

Although not the first issue of paper fiat money in North America, the Continental currency of 1775 issued during the Revolutionary War is well documented as to amount issued and its subsequent depreciation in terms of gold and silver coins. These Continental notes, issued in large quantities for the times, were in direct competition with about $10 million in gold and silver coins. As Gresham's Law suggests, these latter soon disappeared from circulation as the various issues of paper money (private bank issues, certificates, Colonial notes, and bills of credit) made their appearance.

In January 1777 the Continental Congress requested the thirteen State legislatures to declare Continental bills a legal tender. From this time on, paper issues lost their stability in terms of specie, note issues increased, and there was a steady depreciation of the paper Continental.

However, the Continental — unlike the British "paper pound" or the modern Federal Reserve note — was convertible into gold and silver, and it maintained convertibility even while depreciating. One typical bill, by way of example, contained the following inscription:

> The United Colonies. Three dollars. This bill entitles the bearer to receive three Spanish milled dollars, or the value thereof in gold or silver, according to the Resolutions of the Congress, held at Philadelphia, the 10th of May, 1775. Continental Currency.

In spite of this promise to pay in gold and silver coin and the patriotic appeal of the Continental bill, depreciation was rapid and complete. Within six years of issue the Continental note was worthless, or "Not worth a Continental" as the saying became known.

---

*Ibid., p. 24.

TABLE 2-1: VALUE OF CONTINENTAL NOTES IN SILVER COIN

Date	Total Notes Issued	Approximate Value per $1.00 of Silver Coin		
		Webster	Del Mar	
November 1775	$5 million	—	$1.00	in Continental notes
November 1776	19.5 "	1.00	1.00	in Continental notes
November 1777	31.5 "	3.00	3.00	in Continental notes
November 1778	86.0 "	6.00	6.34	in Continental notes
November 1779 (no more issued)	226.0 "	32-45.00	26.00	in Continental notes
November 1780	226.0 "	80-100.00	73.00	in Continental notes

Source: Alexander Del Mar, *The History of Money in America*, (Hawthorne: Omni, 1966).

The decline of paper was hastened by imported French silver crowns and gold "louis." In 1780 French troops fighting in the Revolutionary War bought local supplies with specie. These purchases in gold were in competition with American purchasing agents, who were buying with Government paper money. The state agent of Virginia reported that specie "draws supplies to them [the French] from great distances,"* while another agent reported:

> That infatuating metal will immediately have such influence that not an ounce of any kind of supplies will be furnished to the State agents. The people will go through thick and thin to get the crowns and louis d'or. I forsee the most dangerous consequences arising from these separate interests. The American army must infallibly suffer.†

Exchange values of the Continental varied in different parts of the country. The table above lists values given in del Mar and in Webster for the city of Philadelphia. On December 25, 1779 the Continental exchanged at 35 to 1 for specie in New England,

---

*William Graham Sumner, *The Financier and the Finances of the French Revolution*, (New York: Dodd, Mead, 1892), Volume Two, p. 142.
†*Ibid.*

New York, the Carolinas, and Georgia, but at 40 to 1 in Pennsylvania, New Jersey, Delaware, Maryland, and Virginia. Usually Virginia lagged a month or so behind the falling Philadelphia quotations.

For a year or so the Continental bill was exchangeable into specie at par, declining slowly through 1777 and 1778, then more rapidly as people hastened to pass on bills and hoard specie. By 1779 and 1780 paper fell from 12 to 1 to 100 to 1. In May 1781 the bill ceased to circulate as money and was changed only as a speculation at from 400 to 1000 Continentals for one dollar in gold and silver.

Why did the Congress issue paper fiat money in the first place? Perhaps one member of Congress put it well, expressing the soul of the politician (which hasn't changed very much in the past two hundred years):

> *Do you think, gentlemen, that I will consent to load my constituents with taxes, when we can send to our printer, and get a wagon load of money, one quire of which will pay for the whole?*

The burden of depreciation then, as now, fell on those who had the most (and regrettably misplaced) confidence in the integrity of government. In 1777 these were mostly Whigs, and it was the Whigs who retained paper money, rather than change it for gold and silver. As a result many lost their livelihoods and their fortunes. Those, mostly Tories, who had little confidence in Government or Government paper money, passed the paper bills quickly in trade, and hoarded their specie. And as it is today, those who attempted to protect themselves from Government paper issues "were called Tories, speculators, and many other hard names."

Misunderstanding of the reasons for depreciation of paper bills was as common in 1777 as it is in 1977: "What a shame it is," said a patriotic old lady in 1777, "the Congress should let the poor soldiers suffer, when they have power to make just as much money as they choose."† This is no different in principle from

---

*William M. Gouge, *op. cit.*, Part II, p. 27.
†*Ibid.*, Part II, p. 28.

our modern Congressmen urging the Federal Reserve System to pump credit into the economy to alleviate the sufferings of the unemployed and welfare recipients.

In 1776 Congress observed this depreciation of the Continental bill and in the tradition of King Canute determined to "pass a law" to stop it. If the Continental could not maintain its value by voluntary means, then Congress was determined to maintain its value by compulsion. In the late 1770s Congress had a deep-rooted fixation that it had power over markets and what people would accept as money. So Congress resolved in January 1776 that, "whoever should refuse to receive in payment Continental bills, should be declared and treated as an enemy of his country, and be precluded from intercourse with its inhabitants."

For five years Congress passed all manner of laws, legal tender acts, maximum price laws, and penal laws with heavy penalties, severely enforced, to maintain the value of the Continental bill. As Pelatiah Webster, "an able though not conspicuous citizen of Philadelphia," described it:

> . . . though men of all descriptions stood trembling before this monster of force, without daring to lift a hand against it during all this period, yet its unrestrained energy always proved ineffectual to its purposes, but in every case increased the evils it was designed to remedy, and destroyed the benefits it was intended to promote. . . . Many thousand families of full and easy fortune, were ruined by these fatal measures, and lie in ruins to this day [1790] without the least benefit to the country, or to the great and noble cause in which we were then engaged.*

No more Continentals were issued after 1779. Their value in gold and silver coins continued to decline, reaching about 100 to 1 in late 1780, and ultimately zero value. They were quoted at between 99.5 and 99.9 percent discount in 1781, and accepted at the rate of 100 to 1 in the public debt issue of 1790. It is true that the genuine note issue figures are overstated because British counterfeits infiltrated into the colonies in substantial quantities:

---

*Ibid., p. 29.

The British government promoted the business of counterfeiting extensively, because it was thought that if the credit of the Continental money could be destroyed, the Americans would be obliged to submit, from lack of funds, to maintain their cause.*

If the Continental was an isolated case of specie driving out paper money then perhaps we could give weight to the argument that counterfeits caused depreciation. In fact the Continental is but one example among many examples, each varying somewhat in the conditions but ultimately demonstrating that whenever gold or silver is in competition with paper fiat money, the former will always go into hiding, leaving the field to paper money which will sooner or later deteriorate in value to zero. To quote Webster again:

Thus fell, ended, and died, the Continental currency, aged six years. Bubbles of another sort, such as the Mississippi scheme in France, and the South Sea in England, lasted but a few months, and then burst into nothing; but this held out much longer, and seemed to retain a vigorous constitution to its last: for its circulation was never more brisk than when its exchange was 500 to one; and yet it expired without a groan or struggle. . . .†

The bitter experience of the Continental bill did not go unheeded. The Founders of the United States wrote the lessons of paper fiat money into the Constitution, and Article 1, Section 10 reads: "No State shall . . . make any Thing but gold and silver coin a tender in payment of Debts. . . ." In 1792 Congress adopted a monetary system based only on gold and silver, with no provision whatsoever for paper money. At that time paper money was widely distrusted — for good reason. As Alexander Hamilton commented:

The emitting of paper money is wisely prohibited to the State Governments, and the spirit of the prohi-

---

*Alexander del Mar, *The History of Money in America*, (Hawthorne: Omni, 1966), p. 114.

†William M. Gouge, *op. cit.*, p. 31.

bition ought not to be disregarded by the United State's Government. *

From 1792 to 1977 no Constitutional amendment has affected Article 1, Section 10. Indeed, Supreme Court cases have held that what applies to the States also applies to the Federal Government, thus establishing Alexander Hamilton's observation in case law. Yet in 1976, no gold and silver coins are in circulation; money in the United States is wholly fiat paper.† How we arrived at this position and the efforts being made to maintain our contemporary paper bubble is the story we shall now unfold.

---

*Cited in *Ibid.*, Part II, p. 230.
† For recent court challenges see pp. 90-94 below.

CHAPTER THREE

The Discipline of Gold

> *You shall not crucify mankind upon a cross of gold.*

William Jennings Bryan, 1896.

POLITICIANS AND BUSINESSMEN soon forgot the lessons of those early battles between paper and gold. A common argument in the early nineteenth century was to compare paper money with steam power; paper money, so the argument went, could provide a driving force for the economy, like the steam engine. It would be a force that was not forthcoming from scarce gold and silver. This was an early version of the modern (and equally fallacious) argument that gold is too scarce to provide sufficient liquidity for economic development. These assertions reflect a latent desire to declare money a free good, an impossibility until the utopia arrives when all goods are free. Those who recalled monetary history counseled otherwise. William Gouge in his 1833 classic, *A Short History of Paper Money and Banking in the United States*, pointed out the falsity of the steam engine/paper money analogy: safeguards could prevent accidents to a steam engine, but no safeguards had been devised for accidents with paper money systems. Wrote Gouge:

> *We may amuse ourselves by contriving new modes of paper Banking. We may suppose that a kind of money which has been tried, in various forms, in China,*

Persia, Hindostan, Tartary, Japan, Russia, Sweden, Denmark, Austria, France, Portugal, England, Scotland, Ireland, Canada, the United States, Brazil and Buenos Ayres, and which has everywhere produced mischief, would if we had the control of it, be productive of great good. We may say, it is true that paper money has always produced evil, but it is because it has not been properly managed. But, if there is not something essentially bad in factitious money, there seems to be something in human nature which prevents it being properly managed. No new experiments are wanted to convince mankind of this truth. *

William Gouge wrote this condemnation in 1833, based on the experience of numerous paper money disasters, including those in France, England, and the United States we have described. From 1834 to 1862 William Gouge worked in the U.S. Treasury, on the immediate staff of the Secretary of the Treasury and as adviser to several Democratic administrations. Philosophically in the Jackson-Jefferson laissez-faire tradition, Gouge argued that people used gold and silver as money because, "They found the precious metals had those *specific* qualities which fitted them to be standards and measures of value, and to serve, when in the shape of coin, the purposes of a circulating medium."†

Gouge attributed all the evils of economic fluctuations, speculation, depression and inflation to the use of paper money, citing as evidence the low number of pre-revolutionary (that is, pre-paper money) bankruptcies and the low incidence of bankruptcies in such places as Hamburg and Bremen which were without paper money.

In the last chapter we briefly described the tragic paper-money inflations in France and the United States, and the lesser inflation in England before 1820, which formed the grist for Gouge's thinking and writing. In this chapter we contrast these

---

*William M. Gouge, *A Short History of Paper Money and Banking in the United States (1833)*, (New York: Reprints of Economic Classics, Augustus M. Kelley Publishers, 1968), p. 228 of Part II.

† *Ibid.*, p. 10.

bitter experiences of paper money with the unchallenged reign of the pure gold standard in the nineteenth century.

From 1814, when France adopted the gold Napoleon, and 1821, when Britain went onto a full standard, until 1914, gold ruled supreme as the world's money. During this century the major countries of Europe and the United States progressed from rural backward societies to modern industrial giants. World trade thrived and expanded on a scale not known before. And because the discipline imposed by the gold standard meant that governments could not inflate their currencies, mankind was largely spared the scourge of price inflation with its inevitable sequel, depression. Those minor panics, emphasized in our economic history textbooks, can be traced to bank manipulations of credit and markets or government policy, not to the gold standard *per se*.

Franz Pick has noted the extraordinary stability of the nineteenth century gold standard, compared to the more than 1,500 currency devaluations just in the thirty years from 1946 to 1976. Pick comments that "the so-called golden age of currency stability looks like a fairy tale." Major currencies were on the gold standard as follows:*

French franc	1814-1914	100 years of gold standard stability
Dutch guilder	1816-1914	98 years of gold standard stability
Pound sterling	1821-1914	93 years of gold standard stability
Swiss franc	1850-1936	86 years of gold standard stability
Belgian franc	1832-1914	82 years of gold standard stability
Swedish krona	1873-1931	58 years of gold standard stability
German mark	1875-1914	39 years of gold standard stability
Italian lira	1883-1914	31 years of gold standard stability

What a contrast! Today in 1977 only the heavily gold-backed Swiss franc has any long-run stability. The rest of the world's currencies, including the U.S. dollar, are churning around in competitive devaluations and floating exchange rates, to the despair of investors, export managers, and tourists alike. We have no fixed exchange rates today, and no stability, because fixed exchange rates and stability require the numeraire of gold.

---

*Adapted from Franz Pick, *1975 Pick's Currency Yearbook*, (New York: 21 West Street, 10006, 1975).

The Latin Monetary Union

The Latin Monetary Union was created by France, Belgium, Italy, Switzerland, and Greece in 1865 after a few brief meetings, and is a notable example of how a monetary union *should* work, in contrast to the monetary agreements of today that hold together for a few short months, if that. The main purpose of today's conferences appears to be to provide free junkets to sunny resorts for Treasury officials. (It is worth noting that monetary conferences are *not* held in Reykjavik, Iceland or Dakar, Senegal.)

In any event, these Latin countries back in 1865 minted a gold coin of uniform weight and value with a fineness of .900. Other countries in Europe (Finland and Spain), Asia (Russia and the Philippines), and Latin America (Colombia and Venezuela) subsequently issued gold coins to the specification established by the Latin Monetary Union. The Union's standard was a gold French 100-franc piece, issued between 1855 and 1913, of 32.2580 grams in weight. Similarly, the Colombian 20-peso coin (1859-1877) also weighed 32.2580 grams of .900 fineness. The Belgian 100 francs issued between 1853 and 1912, the Guatamalan 20 pesos (1869-1878), the Greek 100 drachmae (1876), the Italian 100 lire (1832-1927), the Russian 25 roubles (1896-1908), the Swiss 100 francs (1925), and the Venezualen 100 bolivares (1875-1889) were all 32.2580 grams in weight and minted to a fineness of .900. A few coins even used the standard after the dissolution of the Latin Monetary Union in 1926, such as the Albanian 100 francs issued from 1926-1938 and the Liechtenstein 100 franken issued in 1952.

Although not matching the 1000-year life of the Byzantine gold solidus, the French gold 100-franc standard maintained its value for a century — a record not matched by *any* paper currency on record. The Latin Monetary Union was an effective international monetary arrangement, giving monetary stability and facilitating trade for over sixty years. By contrast, compare what happened when these same countries adopted a paper currency after leaving the gold standard. France has had two disasterous inflations since 1914. Greece has seen its paper drachmae drop to zero. Russian paper currency in 1917 and a few years thereafter became valueless, and today's Soviet paper currency is not convertible on the world market. The Italian lira is worth a minute fraction of its former value.

So why not substitute a gold standard union for the flabby Smithsonian paper pact and the patchwork temporary modern agreements? The answer is simple: a gold standard is non-political, and it cannot be manipulated by politicians and academic utopians. Gold is a most effective discipline against fiscal profligacy. There are too many influential drones living off paper money inflation to adopt a stable and equitable monetary system. The only effective way to achieve the stability of the gold standard today is to ignore or bypass the paper standard *individually*, and move to the use of gold coins and gold clauses in contracts.

William Jennings Bryan had an emotional electioneering phrase, "You shall not crucify mankind upon a cross of gold." But neither Bryan nor any of today's politicians is willing to accept responsibility for the monetary chaos of inflation, deflation, and instability which is latent in paper-debt systems.

While the nineteenth century gold standard experience does suggest that full 100-percent gold backing is not required to achieve monetary stability, so long as we are afflicted with predatory politicians 100-percent backing may be a necessary safeguard. The French franc, which formed the basis for the Latin Monetary Union, circulated side by side with unbacked paper currency. The following table reports the relative quantities of paper and gold in circulation in France and the proportion that specie formed of the total:

TABLE 3-1: PROPORTIONS OF PAPER AND SPECIE IN FRENCH FRANC FROM 1801 TO 1886

Year	Gold and Silver Coin	Paper Money	Total	Percent Specie
1801	2290	30	2320	98.7
1806	2300	65	2365	97.3
1814	2100	25	2125	98.8
1830	2615	225	2840	92.1
1833	2625	215	2840	92.1
1837	2850	204	3054	93.3
1847	2500	240	2740	91.2
1849	2575	435	3010	85.5

1852	2875	670	3545	81.1
1860	3600	750	4350	82.8
1870	3750	1750	5500	68.2
1876	5000	2550	7550	66.2
1886	6000	2800	8800	68.2

Source: Alexander Del Mar, Money and Civilization, (Hawthorne, California: Omni Publications, 1975), p. 290-291.

Up to 1847 specie comprised over 90 percent of circulating francs. It is of interest to note that war and revolution in both the nineteenth and twentieth century bring changes in the paper-gold ratio. The abrupt change in the specie proportion in the 1849 French franc was a reflection of the 1848 European Revolution. The drop from 82 percent to 68 percent in the decade of the 1860s reflected war and preparations for war. War in 1914 meant the suspension of the gold standard, but in 1849 and 1870 it brought only partial substitution of paper for gold.

This European tradition of gold coinage and substantial gold backing for note issues (until 1914) was not repeated as uniformly or as emphatically in the United States. Gold-producing California maintained a note-free gold coin circulation until 1870, but paper issues were a more significant part of the nineteenth century American monetary tradition.

The American Experience with Gold

Relatively few gold coins circulated in the United States up to 1830 because the U.S. Treasury underpriced gold and this naturally encouraged export of coins. (See p. 117.) From 1830 until mid-century both banknotes and gold coin circulated in the eastern United States, while in gold-producing California almost all circulation prior to the Civil War was gold coin. Some were issued by the Federal Mint; even more in the 1840s and 50s came from private mints; and some barely constitutional gold bars issued by the State Assay Office were used as coin. Californians objected to the use of Federal "Greenbacks" issued in the Civil War and San Francisco merchants independently decided to stay on the gold standard. Private competition by California minters with government mints was halted in 1864, but as late as

1914 the U.S. Treasury was still trying to halt circulation of private gold pieces in San Francisco.

It is worth recording that private gold coin issues in California and Colorado maintained higher standards than the competing Federal government issues. One example is the 1860-1861 gold coins minted by Clark, Gruber & Co., a Denver, Colorado banking firm, which coined eagles, half-eagles, and quarter-eagles. These were alloyed at government standards but coined one percent heavier than the Federal issue, to protect the user from metal loss by abrasion while the coin was in circulation. Would that governments were as careful with their reputations! The reason for this high minting standard is obvious. A private firm's survival depends on its reputation, and its reputation in the field of private coins depends on giving full gold weight. A government can ignore fears about its reputation; there is no requirement to give full weight because it can always use the police power of the state to enforce legal tender laws. This experience suggests that a return to private coinage, as circulated in California and Colorado in the mid-nineteenth century, would restore intrinsic value and honesty to money.

The Civil War brought the United States to its first suspension of convertibility and its first inconvertible paper fiat currency. (The Continental bill was always convertible into gold and silver, even while sinking in value.) In 1861 several events — a drain on bank reserves stemming from Treasury loans, military reverses, the threat of war with England, the probability of a large Treasury deficit — all combined to encourage a run on the banks. Drained of gold reserves, the banking system suspended payment of coin for paper and the United States left the gold standard from 1862 to 1879. In 1862 Congress authorized issue of a paper currency, the so-called "Greenbacks," and by the end of the Civil War a total of $450 million in paper notes was outstanding. From the outset the paper greenback was traded at a discount to gold. Thanks to the inflation such paper money brought, living costs doubled in the last three years of the Civil War.*

The International Monetary Conference of 1867, in which the U.S. was a prominent participant, universally accepted the

---

*Irwin Unger, *The Greenback Era*, (New Jersey: Princeton, 1964).

gold standard. Subsequently, Congress passed a law fixing the weight of the gold dollar at 1.61290 milligrams, "to establish a permanent line of monetary unity spanning the Christian world from San Francisco to the confines of Constantinople."* However, until 1879 the U.S. dollar was still divorced from gold; and the fiat paper dollar depreciated heavily in terms of gold and sterling, which was still linked to gold. In 1879 the U.S. returned to the gold standard; convertibility and fixed exchange rates were followed by an era of relative stability and industrial expansion.

Looking at the nineteenth century as a whole, it is notable that the business cycles were short but in each case (1819-1820, 1839-1843, 1857-1860, 1873-1878, 1893-1897) they were preceded by government easy-money policies. Thus, a government-sponsored boom was followed by a decline in economic activity. The same pattern holds in the twentieth century in 1920-1921, 1929-1933, and in the years since World War II under Keynesian "fine-tuning" of the economy.

The official view of gold in the U.S. monetary system differs as night from day, depending on whether you are reading statements written before or after 1960. Prior to 1960, gold was described as the center of the American monetary system. According to the 1947 edition of the official booklet describing the work of the Federal Reserve System,† "Gold is the ultimate basis of Federal Reserve credit . . . ." The booklet continues, "In the American monetary system the standard dollar is defined as a weight of gold."

Until 1961 the Federal Reserve System recognized that international balances were settled by gold; as stated in the Federal Reserve booklet quoted above, "Movements of gold from one country to another are the ultimate means by which international balances are settled."‡ International balances due could be settled either by borrowing funds in the United States, by drawing on dollar deposits, or by claiming gold from the United States. The latter was the settlement of last resort and normally

---

*Quoted in Walter T. K. Nugent, *Money and American Society 1865-1880*, (New York: The Free Press, 1968).

† Board of Governors of the Federal Reserve System, *The Federal Reserve System: Purposes and Functions*, (Washington, D.C.: Federal Reserve System, 1947, Second edition).

‡ *Ibid.*, p. 104.

consisted of "earmarking" gold for that country's account at the Federal Reserve Bank vaults in New York. Rarely was gold actually shipped out of the country; this usually occurred only on occasions reflecting international political distrust.*

From 1934, when President Franklin Delano Roosevelt revalued gold, until 1948 gold flowed into the United States. This reflected the healthy U.S. balance-of-payments position. But since 1948 gold has moved out of the United States, and heavily so in the 1960s. In traditional monetary practice, an outflow of gold obviously decreases the reserves of the United States, and where the law required a gold backing (40 percent in 1914, 25 percent from World War II until rescinded by President Johnson in 1968), declining reserves restrict the ability to supply notes and create deposits. The compensating effect leads to declining imports and expanding exports to correct the trade deficit and reduce the gold outflow.

It is this disciplinary function of gold that is irksome to politicians and managed-economy bureaucrats and academicians. Politicians are always eager to buy votes with promises of perpetual prosperity, and bureaucrats are happy to go along to expand their own empire building. Consequently, under the more recent influence of the "something for nothing" philosophy, official statements are designed to avoid or disparage the discipline of gold:

> *The Federal Reserve's financial strength and authority is such today that it is in a position to offset, when desirable, the credit and monetary effects of any likely movements of gold.†*

What this means is that when the politicians face an election ("when desirable"), they can ignore the signals of an outflow of gold, override the automatic controls ("in a position to offset"), and pump in more credit and notes (to eliminate the undesirable "credit and monetary effects of any likely movements of gold").

One of the phony rationales used by our collectivist empire builders for these procedures is that sufficient gold does not exist

---

*In 1975, for example, the Arabs removed their gold from New York vaults.
†*Ibid.*, p. 106.

and we need "more liquidity." This common criticism is usually phrased as, "There isn't enough gold in the world to have a monetary system based on gold." Even an official voice for capitalism, *Business Week* magazine, accepted this fallacy when it said, "At $100 an oz., gold literally is too expensive to use for money."* Now, the editors of *Business Week* and competent economists know better than this. The quantity of gold in existence is irrelevant. What is relevant is the price of gold. At a market price for gold there is, by definition, sufficient gold to supply all demand, including monetary uses. That is the first principle of supply and demand taught in any Economics 1A course. Yet it is extraordinary how many otherwise well-informed economists (who presumably have taught Economics 1A) and financial commentators claim to accept this canard. (See p. 108 below for the simple theoretical analysis.) In fact, it is precisely *because* gold can command higher market clearing prices that it has useful qualities as a monetary reserve: price reflects scarcity, and scarcity is a restraint on monetary abuse. There is no scarcity of paper money, and consequently there is no restraint on its issue. Hence inflation. It may be that modern economists have tried to bury the Quantity Theory of Money, but their wishes or pretenses have not changed economic reality.

Of course, a market clearing price for gold (assuming a 100-percent cover for all present paper debts), might suggest a price of $800 to $1,000 an ounce.† This would be a pleasant windfall for those with the foresight to own gold, but it would mean psychological devastation for those who have built their careers on the philosophy of helping everyone to live at the expense of everyone else. The latter need to conduct an anti-gold crusade for their own self-preservation.

The Totalitarian Assault on Gold

The reader may well ask the question: why, if gold has the ability to provide stability, do we have the persistent propaganda

---

*May 19, 1973.

†On this question of a gold price, see American Institute for Economic Research, *Is There an Upper Limit to the Price of Gold?*, December 1973. The report concludes that, on the basis of historical exchange values with pig iron and copper from 1850 to 1934, the price of gold should range from $245 to $345 per ounce.

for paper fiat systems — particularly when the end result has always been economic chaos? We have already suggested the politician as one culprit, but bankers, economists, and academicians are equally to blame.

When we project early monetary experience to modern times it should not surprise us to learn that *all* totalitarian societies, from John Law's France to Hitler's Third Reich and Stalin's Soviet empire, have conducted a war on gold. Indeed, the individual sovereignty granted by gold ownership *must* be removed as an essential prerequisite for an authoritarian regime. Gold grants sovereignty. In a dictatorship all vestiges of sovereignty have to be consolidated in the hands of the ruling elite.

An early example is banker John Law's paper-money system in eighteenth century France. After initiating a personal bank based on paper money, rather than specie, Law was invited by the French court to institute a similar scheme, the Banque Royale, to use his system for "the good of France" — in this case, the authoritarian French court. While our present system is subject to the whims of politicians, John Law's scheme was subject to royal caprice. Printers worked overtime and paper money was forced by law on French citizens. When the French people protested, Law proposed to the regent, "People must be compelled to accept paper money."* Thus specie was prohibited to be moved into certain French towns, and it was forbidden to give or accept silver or copper coins over a certain limited amount. Just before the paper bubble burst, unwelcome reality intruded. Perceptive observers realized that the value of the Banque Royale paper that had been issued could not be covered by all the specie in the world, let alone France. The "realizers" quietly began to cash in, converting their paper into diamonds and gold and real estate, and then fading into the woodwork.

Consequently, in the eighteenth century John Law adopted a course that would be copied 200 years later by former-banker turned Treasury Secretary William Simon; he declared war on gold, to maintain a paper money monopoly. By royal decree, paper money was declared to be at a premium in comparison to gold. When people ignored the decree, attempts were made to

---

*Georges Oudard, *The Amazing Life of John Law*, (New York: Payson & Clarke, 1928), p. 203.

control prices. Above all, John Law had to maintain *confidence* in paper issues. Nevertheless, the more Law attacked gold, the more people converted paper into gold. When gold went into hiding, paper-money holders converted their notes into *anything* of intrinsic value: jewels, clothing, food, even books. As Law's biographer, Georges Oudard, commented: "Lagrange, one of the most famous among them [the "realizers"] bought up one entire issue of Bayle's Dictionary, for want of anything better."*

When Law's wife confirmed that a Paris shopkeeper had asked for 1,000 paper livres for cloth worth 360 gold livres,

> *Law had the foolish man sent for, and explained to him that there was only one currency in the kingdom and that paper money was the equivalent of gold. "No," said the man. "Burn my cloth and you will find there is still something left afterwards. But if I burn one of your 1,000 livre notes, all that remains is just a little ash."†*

The U.S. Treasury since 1960 has repeated many of John Law's efforts to maintain confidence in paper and to demonetize gold. And contemporary "realizers" are once again at work. The "gold bug" of today is acutely aware of the paper money fallacy — and takes practical steps to invest in more tangible gold and silver.

The famous French statesman Talleyrand in 1790, as we noted earlier, posed the problem for the paper totalitarians quite succinctly:

> *You can arrange a society so that a man shall be forced to take a thousand livres in paper instead of a thousand livres in specie, but you can never arrange society so that a man shall be obliged to give a thousand livres in specie for a thousand livres in paper.*

In brief, you may coerce people to take paper money in payment for goods and services, but you can never successfully coerce them to give up gold in exchange for paper. Why not? Because people will hoard gold rather than part with it.

---

*Ibid., p. 255.
*Ibid., p. 254.

As in Law's time, current politico-economic ideas such as Keynesianism, which require the surrender of individual economic power and sovereignty, work best in totalitarian societies. And they require the elimination of gold as a medium of exchange to be effective. Keynes himself pointed out this relationship in an understandably little-known preface to the German edition of his *General Theory*. In Keynes' own words:

> *The theory of aggregate production ... nevertheless can be much easier adapted to the conditions of the total state than the theory of production and distribution of a given production put forth under conditions of free competition and a great amount of laissez-faire.*

The Nazi state which Keynes had in mind when writing the above preface also declared war on gold. In this instance it came as the final stage in the proposed Nazi program of world domination, rather than as a preliminary step. On July 25, 1940 Reichsbank president Walter Funk outlined the Hitlerite *New Economic Order* and asserted that the U.S. gold stock in Fort Knox (then valued at $20 billion) would become worthless. There is a remarkable parallel between this Nazi effort to establish a "world order," with five or six regional economies, and the present effort pushed by the Jimmy Carters and the Trilateralists in the U.S. to achieve a "new world order" with regional groupings.*

The assault on gold today is an integral part of a planned move into a new economic order under the dominance of a single country. It was Nazi Germany in the 1940s; it is the United States in the 1970s. In brief, the war on gold that we observe today, and discuss below, is dollar imperialism, designed to maintain the U.S. dollar as the *only* world currency without competitors. † The purpose is the formation of a world totalitarian state under Wall Street dominance.

The so-called "dictatorship of the proletariat" in the Soviet

---

*See *Foreign Affairs*, April 1974, "The Hard Road to World Order."

†The reader who wishes to pursue the question of the relationship between the State and fiat money should read Ludwig von Mises, *Human Action — A Treatise on Economics*, (London: William Hodges and Company, Limited, 1949), and *The Theory of Money and Credit*, (New York: The Foundation for Economic Education, Inc., 1971).

Union has taken an eminently practical approach to gold. Although gold was condemned by Lenin as a worthless relic of capitalism, fit only to be used for lining toilets, his successor, Stalin, recognized the contribution of the 1849 California gold rush to American industrial development. According to reputable reporters,* Stalin decided to introduce the same gold mechanism to advance Soviet socialism.

While today gold is absolutely forbidden to Soviet citizens, Russian newly mined gold is a major means of purchasing the foreign technology that is vitally needed to shore up the inefficient economy and to expand the military power of the U.S.S.R. In 1975, while the U.S. was embarked on an anti-gold crusade, the Soviet Union confirmed its faith in gold, for its own external use, by issuing its first gold coin since 1923. The re-issue of the Chervonetz ten-ruble piece, with 0.2489 troy ounces of fine gold, was available for foreign purchase only. The eminently practical Soviets have found gold to be a double-edged weapon to build a totalitarian society and to advance Soviet-style imperialism. Internally, the sovereignty inherent in gold is denied to the Russian people. Externally, the universal acceptance of gold is used to purchase technology and food to overcome the internal deficiencies of an unfree society.

A totalitarian new world order is likely to be the coming sad fate of the once bright and promising American dream. A society that commenced with libertarian ideas and limited government is degenerating into a totalitarian nightmare, and the war on gold is a necessary device to impose this totalitarian state. U.S. policy is to phase out gold, the dollar's competitor, from the world economic system. This monopoly goal is planned as a long-term, gradual process. No doubt at some time in the future, under the pressure of economic events, gold will reassert itself and the establishment elite will have a choice: either adopt the discipline of gold or resort to naked force to impose a paper fiat dollar on both American citizens and the world at large. The history of totalitarian elites suggests that the use of force will be chosen over the right of the people to decide for themselves what they want to use as money.

---

*John D. Littlepage, *In Search of Soviet Gold*, (London: George G. Harrap, 1939), pp. 37-9.

We can aptly conclude this discussion of gold as a protector of individual sovereignty and the reason for the assault on gold with a quotation from F. A. von Hayek:

> *With the exception only of the period of the gold standard, practically all governments of history have used their exclusive power to issue money to defraud and plunder the people. What is dangerous and ought to be eliminated is not the government's right to issue money, but its exclusive right to do so and its power to force people to accept that money at a particular rate.**

In brief, individual liberty can only be guaranteed under a gold standard with no monopoly power over money issues. That is what the discipline of gold is all about.

---

*Reported from a speech in Lausanne by *Gold Newsletter*, (Volume IV, No. 120, December 1975).

CHAPTER FOUR

Inflation Balloons After 1920

> *Of all the contrivances for cheating the laboring classes of mankind, none has been more effective than that which deludes them with paper money.*

Daniel Webster.

> *Up to this day it has never yet been demonstrated that any agency can be invented to which power to govern the currency could be entrusted without ultimately disastrous consequences.*

Adolph Miller, member Federal Reserve Board; quoted in Percy L. Greaves, Jr., *Understanding the Dollar Crisis*, (Boston: Western Islands, 1973), p. 231.

THE WORLD MONETARY SCENE in 1977 is unique in all of human history: *all* countries are on a paper fiat standard, and only a handful of currencies (for instance the Swiss franc) are even remotely tied to the discipline of gold. The undisciplined inflation of the money supply has led the world to double- and triple-digit price increases, and we have daily reminders of Ludwig von Mises' classic pithy remark:

> *Government is the only agency that can take a useful commodity like paper, slap some ink on it, and make it totally worthless.*

In the United States, the Federal Reserve System is a private monopoly of legal tender granted by Congress and upheld by the Courts, rather than a government monopoly as in France or Germany. Inflation of the note issue is solely the responsibility of the Federal Reserve, as is the manipulation and expansion of the gigantic debt pyramid (that is, purchasing power created by banks with bookkeeping or computer entries). Note issue and debt creation are the sole causes of inflation; all the other so-called "causes" of price increases are merely symptoms. The sad consequences of John Law, La Banque Generale in France, the assignats, the Continental bills, and other illustrations which spell out the inevitable consequence of monetary inflation, are recorded but ignored. These valid historical reminders to the contrary, the post-1920 period has witnessed extraordinary inflations and in 1977 we cannot avoid more price increases.*

In previous chapters, we have recorded the issue of assignats, paper pounds, and Continental bills, and the price increases which followed. We noted that the issue of paper Greenbacks in the Civil War led to a doubling of price levels. After the 1920s, most governments, under ideological pressure, discarded the discipline of gold, increased the money supply for political purposes, and so generated an era of awesome price increases. Inflation, then, is a *political*, not an economic, problem. Political decisions are made to increase the money supply or to introduce policies requiring an expansion of the money supply, and the resultant expansion creates upward movements in the price levels. It is political intervention into the economic system — in short, socialism — that creates inflation. A pure laissez-faire system would (barring extraordinary increases in the supply of gold) result in a gently falling price level. Yet so twisted is modern political reasoning that the free enterprise market is blamed for inflation, along with most of the other social and economic ills of mankind!

---

*The term "inflation" is generally used today to refer to price increases. But traditionally the word "inflation" means an increase in the money supply. It is fundamental, however we use the term, to understand that every price inflation has been preceded by an increase in the money supply. Even an increase in the supply of gold will lead to price increases, and has. Today's money managers must ignore the Quantity Theory of Money and deliberately blur the distinction made above, because their predominant objective is political. Tackling the *fundamentals* of price increases will make these political objectives unattainable.

"But Gold Is Too Scarce . . . ."

Stemming from the political root of inflation is the peculiar non-economic nature of the contemporary argument against gold. The typical anti-gold argument is to the effect that gold is "too scarce" to act as money or, in more technical terms, gold cannot provide "sufficient" liquidity for expanding a domestic economy or world trade.

The post-1920 attempt to substitute a paper money and debt system for the gold standard originated in Resolution 9 of the 1922 Genoa Conference. This Resolution recommended introduction of the gold *exchange* standard, which "makes for savings in the use of gold by maintaining reserves in the form of foreign balances." But a gold-exchange standard is *not* the same thing as a gold standard. The use of foreign currencies as reserves equal to gold opened another door to the present inflationary chaos. Even well-informed sources have fallen into the trap of confusing a gold-exchange standard (post-1922) with a full gold standard (pre-1914).*

Presented under the guise of "improving" the world's monetary system, the Genoa Conference had as its major purpose phasing out gold from the world's monetary scene. A rather similar system had been imposed on India in 1898, allowing gold to be used only for external settlements. In 1922, to "economize" in the use of gold, both sterling and the dollar were arbitrarily held to be equal to gold.

Students of the development of the "new world order" will be fascinated by the presence of Round Table members at the 1922 Conference; indeed, they claim to have done most of the work of the Conference. Less than a decade later, the Chatham House Study Group of the Royal Institute of International Affairs (the "front door" of the Round Table) assembled a conference on the international functions of gold. A paper, "How to economize gold," by Sir Otto Niemeyer, occupied a prominent position in the conference.† In it Niemeyer made the assertion:

---

*See, for example, Merrill Lynch, Pierce, Fenner & Smith, Inc., *Gold — A Special Study*, (New York: 1973), p. 1: "Britain's return to the gold standard at an overvalued exchange rate ended in disaster." This confusion of the traditional gold standard with a gold *exchange* standard suggests an inability to get to the root of the gold-vs.-debt problem.

†Royal Institute of International Affairs, *The International Gold Problem*, (London: Oxford Press, 1931).

*I therefore feel very strongly that it is very impor-
tant to establish a general view that a gold coin in internal circulation is not a sign of good form or of advanced
economic conditions, but just the opposite — it is the
sign of almost medieval decadence.* *

Perhaps we can understand why banker Niemeyer and the
Royal Institute for International Affairs, with their own peculiar
political purposes, wanted gold declared "too scarce" to use as
money. It is much more difficult to understand why as competent an economist as R. G. Hawtrey falls into the trap of discuss-
ing a "scarcity of gold."†

Bring a Suitcase for Your Paycheck

During the inter-war period, the fear of gold as money was
the fear of price deflation — something no banker looks upon
favorably. But it was inflation that should have claimed attention. The German hyper-inflation of 1923, the best known of
these inflations,‡ was an event of uncalculated significance. The
collapse of the mark brought untold misery to millions, wiped out
the German middle class, and was a major factor in the rise of Hit-
lerism.

A German 1875 law had provided for an "elastic" note issue
and was framed by the same German banking interests that do-
nated Paul Warburg to the United States — the same Warburg
who was the brainchild and architect of the Federal Reserve Act
of 1913, with its "elastic" note issue. The German monetary system had no legal gold reserve requirement for its notes; the
Federal Reserve System started out with a 40-percent reserve
which has now been reduced to zero.

In 1914, when Germany went to war, the Reichsbank note
circulation was 2,904 million marks backed by 2,092 million
marks of gold. At the end of the war in 1918 it was 22,188 million marks, still backed by over 2,000 million in gold. Under the

---

*Ibid., p. 86.

† See p. 147 below for an economic analysis of the concept of a "scarcity of gold."

‡See Constantino Bresciani-Turroni, *The Economics of Inflation*, (New York, Kelley,
1968), and Fritz K. Ringer, *The German Inflation of 1923*, (New York: Oxford, 1969).

pressure of reparations imposed by Wall Street, the German government resorted to the printing press. By 1923 the note issue was increasing by 250 billion marks a week, against a minute gold reserve of 467 million marks. At the end of 1923 the dollar exchange rate was 2.27 U.S. cents for *one billion* German marks. The mark depreciated hourly. The most frenetic daily activity consisted of turning paper marks into *anything* of tangible value. Here is how the situation was described by a former editor of *Frankfurter Zeitung*:

> *Large laundry baskets filled with paper money had to be carried into the editorial conference room where the editors would sort it out, count it, and distribute the pay.*
>
> *As soon as somebody got his bundle, he'd rush out to buy whatever he could. Anything was more valuable than money. More and more people turned to speculation and blackmarketing in cloth, precious metals, foreign bills and so on. The result was that the output of industry sagged.*
>
> *Because of price controls and rationing, goods were scarce in the cities. Foraging in the countryside became commonplace. The railroad stations were jammed with people going out to the peasants to bargain for food.* *

This tragic phenomenon was repeated after World War II in 1945-1946, when the German note issue was 44,704 million marks and the gold backing only 21 million gold marks. Paper currency again became worthless and Germans resorted to barter with cigarettes, soap, and coffee as the most acceptable forms of money.

Other European paper currencies have gone down the same drain: the Hungarian pengo, the Greek drachma, the French franc in the recent past, the Italian lire and the British pound today. When we look at today's gold reserves in the major European central banks, we find that the central banks which have increased their gold reserves in recent decades are in those same countries that experienced dramatic hyper-inflation in the past.

---

*U.S. News and World Report, December 24, 1973.

The Threshold of World Hyper-inflation

Looking around the monetary world in 1977, inflation is the most important economic problem. In many countries any increase in gross national product is immediately eaten up by price increases. In Argentina, for instance, where President Isabel Peron was replaced by a military junta, price inflation has been running at a rate of 600 percent per annum. With this amount of inflation, normal economic activity comes to a standstill; the country teeters on the brink of economic collapse. Inflation in Europe, even in mid-depression, has been running at double-digit rates (43 percent in Iceland, around 15-25 percent in England, in France well above the government target of nine percent, even Switzerland has felt price increases of 3.4 percent per annum).

Nowhere in Europe is a gold reserve proportionately large enough to act as a real discipline or brake on prices. Iceland has a mere 1.7 percent gold backing. (See Table 4-1.) The largest gold reserve is held by West Germany, the equivalent of 8.0 percent of the money stock, yet there are significant price increases in that country. These conditions all support the nineteenth century experience: while gold reserves can be a partial brake on price increases, only a 100-percent gold-backed currency, with no substantial debt issues, will guarantee stable prices and exchange rates.

TABLE 4-1: COMPARATIVE INCREASES IN 1975 CONSUMER PRICES IN OECD COUNTRIES

	Percent Rate of Price Inflation 1975	Percent Gold Reserves of Money Stock (M1)
ICELAND	43.6	1.7
UNITED KINGDOM	25.0	3.0
ITALY	11.2	4.2
FRANCE	9.6	5.0
UNITED STATES	7.6	4.2
GERMANY	5.4	8.0
SWITZERLAND	3.4	6.3

Source: International Monetary Fund. Money stock is approximately M1 of the Federal Reserve System.

CHART 4-1: MONEY SUPPLY AND INFLATION IN THE U.S.

Annual percent change in U.S. money supply compared to annual percent change in U.S. Consumer Price Index

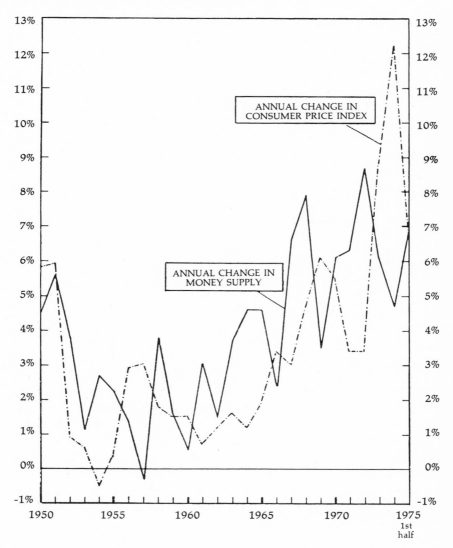

Source: J. Aron, *Gold Statistics and Analysis, October 1975,* (New York: J. Aron & Company, Inc., 1975)

The trend in both money supply and price increases in the United States is brought out dramatically in Chart 4-1. The annual change in money supply is plotted, along with the annual changes in the consumer price index. The overall trend is strongly upwards, with upward sweeps in prices lagging behind upward surges in the money supply.

What is the ultimate significance of this upward trend in money supply and so in future prices? No one has stated the final outcome better than Ludwig von Mises:

> *Inflationism is not a variety of economic policies. It is an instrument of destruction; if not stopped very soon, it destroys the market entirely. . . . Inflationism cannot last; if not radically stopped in time, it must inexorably lead to a complete breakdown. It is an expedient of people who do not care a whit for the future of their nation and its civilization. It is Madam de Pompadour's policy:* Après nous le deluge.*

Gold: The Asset of Last Resort

Those entrapped by the herd instinct are drowned in the deluges of history. But there are always the few who observe, reason, and take precautions, and thus escape the flood. For these few gold has been the asset of last resort for inflation.

Gold is the traditional store of wealth in times of inflation and monetary turmoil, and the use of gold as the asset of last resort continues in the 1970s. Almost every exchange crisis or price surge jiggles the gold price upward, as demand increases for a portable store of wealth. During the long-drawn-out involvement in Vietnam, those Vietnamese who could see the defeat of a demoralized United States at the end of the road quietly turned their assets into *taels*. These are thin gold strips, weighing about one ounce each, manufactured in Hong Kong and Singapore. Large numbers of such taels were later sold in the U.S. refugee camps at Camp Pendleton, Fort Chaffee, Eglin Air Force Base, Indiantown Gap Military Reservation, and at the refugee camp on

---

*American Opinion, March 1967.

Guam. One firm, U.S. Silver, handled about one-third of the esti-mated $15 million sales of gold and estimated the total export of gold taels at about $250 million.* So while the U.S. Treasury is attempting to demonetize gold and phase it out of the monetary system, a very practical demonstration of the age-old reliance on gold as an asset of last resort was in progress in the U.S. govern-ment's own institutions!

Moreover, at the government level itself several examples can be cited of the use of gold as collateral for loans of last resort. When government paper money is unacceptable and worthless, banks and foreign governments will still lend against gold collateral. Portugal's internal financial and economic chaos, stem-ming from uncertain political conditions, brought Portugal to the door of bankruptcy in 1975. But Portugal had continuously accumulated gold, and had a $4.2 billion reserve. Part was used as collateral for a $250 million standby credit from the Bank for International Settlements. A $150 million Eurobank loan from Morgan Guaranty and First National City Bank of New York was also collateralized with part of the gold hoard.† And the directors of these prestigious Wall Street enterprises are the very same di-rectors responsible for the cry that gold is an outmoded relic that should be phased out of the system! If gold is so worthless why its favored use as collateral?

In February 1976 Portugal obtained another $250 million loan, this time from West Germany. Again, gold was used as collateral. Portugal, like other countries, retains its gold in the vaults and raises loans with gold as collateral, rather than sell any of its gold reserves on the market. The inference is obvious: A loan can be paid off in paper fiat money, but once gold is sold there is no surety it will ever return.

Another country that recently saved itself from disaster by using its gold reserves is once-prosperous and glamorous Uruguay. Before World War II Uruguay enjoyed one of the best standards of living in South America, a high literacy rate, and a reasonably stable developing economy. Then came the welfare state! As early as 1956, the *Manchester Guardian* had called Uruguay, ". . . the sad spectacle of a sick Welfare State." One

---

Coin World, November 19, 1975.
†*Business Week*, October 27, 1975, p. 40.

citizen in three was a "public servant," there were constant
strikes, and Uruguay faced a huge foreign payments deficit. By
the late 1960s the deficit had increased many times, capital fled
the country, 50 percent of a paycheck was taken for "social benefits," and almost half the population was dependent on the
government for its income. The monetary system was in chaos. In
1950 the Uruguayan peso was the most solid currency in Latin
America, worth U.S. $0.50. The rate depreciated as follows:

1950	1 peso	=	0.50 cents U.S.
1961	1 peso	=	0.09 cents U.S.
1965	1 peso	=	0.01 cents U.S.
1968	1 peso	=	0.005 cents U.S.

Price increases stem from an increase in the money supply.
In Uruguay the money supply went from 2.9 million pesos in
1961 to 27.5 million pesos in 1972. Interest rates ranged up to 50
percent by the end of the 1960s. By 1975 Uruguay was in des-
perate need of a foreign loan, but had a totally depreciated, worthless paper currency. A loan was raised from a consortium of European bankers with gold as collateral. Uruguay had retained sufficient grip on reality to maintain a gold reserve; 940,000 ounces
(valued at $117 an ounce) were pledged for a loan of $110 million.

A small African gold producer, Ghana, moved its gold refining and sales operations from London to Zurich as part of its
collateral for a Swiss loan.*

In September 1974, Italy borrowed $2,000 million from West
Germany against gold collateral valued at $120 an ounce.

The dangers of *not* having a gold reserve are exemplified in
the case of Great Britain and the failing pound. In 1974 *Reuters*
reported:

> *Kuwaiti commercial banks have recently begun —
> albeit cautiously — converting part of their reserves into*

---

*Timothy Green, *The World of Gold Today*, (New York: Walker and Company,
1973).

gold, something they have not done before, according to banking sources here. Previously, the banks had preferred to invest mainly in West European and North American currencies, or more traditional alternatives such as real estate. Now they consider it desirable to hold between 5% and 10% of their assets in gold, the sources said.*

What has Kuwait got to do with Great Britain and the pound sterling? This shift to a pro-gold stance in Kuwait was followed in 1975 by Kuwait's refusal to accept paper sterling in payment for oil imports to Great Britain. No gold, no oil.

Why is gold acceptable as an asset of last resort? To be used as a store of value or medium of exchange, a commodity must have qualities known to a large number of persons. Above all there must be the expectation of a generally recognized scale of values within society at large, so that when the time comes to recoup the values inherent in the monetary commodity others will be there, ready and willing to exchange desired goods for the asset held. Gold has always fulfilled this role, without question or hesitation. Gold is established as such a commodity because of its unique physical properties — properties not held by any other commodity: it is durable, it is scarce, and it requires resources to acquire it (in other words, the supply of gold cannot suddenly be increased). By contrast, paper money can be increased in any quantity, by the simple device of shifting figures on the face of a bank note or even by creating additional credit in an IBM computer. There is no assurance of scarcity, consequently the quantity available is always in doubt. As a store of value, gold is also unique in that it cannot deteriorate or be destroyed. All the gold mined in history is still in existence.

The Acid Test of Value

Lest there be any remaining skeptics and doubters among our readers, the inflation of the twentieth century presents an acid

---

*Reuters, February 28, 1974. Quoted in James Dines, *The Invisible Crash*, (New York: Random House, 1975), p. 341.

test of the relative value of gold coins and paper fiat money as a store of value.

Let us suppose the reader had, back in 1914, the choice of investing in a $10 Federal Reserve note or a $10 gold coin (say a Liberty Eagle). What would be the relative gains or losses in the two savings media during the period of 62 years from 1914-1976? Which would better preserve wealth for the future?

By 1976, the purchasing power of the 1914 $10 Federal Reserve paper bill would have shrunk to 1/22nd of its 1914 value, assuming the bill had not been demonetized. The loss of purchasing power is represented by the shaded area in Diagram 4-1. On the other hand, the 1914 $10 Liberty gold coin would have appreciated considerably — even ignoring its numismatic value. A 1914 Liberty $10 Eagle contains 16.7 grams of .900 fine gold, which is worth about $65.00 in today's Federal Reserve notes (calculating bullion at $130 per troy ounce). Certainly $65.00 does not fully reflect the loss of purchasing power of $10 since 1914, but gold bullion has not yet fully reflected the loss of purchasing power. If bullion were closer to $400 an ounce, the $10 Eagle would then fully compensate for the loss of purchasing power as represented in terms of paper fiat money. Taking the numismatic value into account, a common date $10 Eagle would be worth about $110.00 in Federal Reserve notes. Obviously, the gold investor in 1914 would have preserved his wealth, while the paper note investor lost his.*

Another method of measuring the relative decline in purchasing power of the Federal Reserve note is the market price of silver dollars. A bag of 1,000 silver Morgan dollars, face value $1,000, is quoted today at about $3,000 per bag. In other words, if our 1914 investor had chosen ten silver dollars in 1914 instead of ten paper Federal Reserve notes he would still have come out ahead (again, ignoring numismatic values). One interesting point about silver dollars is that the Internal Revenue Service values these coins today at face value — that is, one dollar. This presents the intriguing possibility of conducting transactions, say in real

---

*An alternative would be to invest in interest-bearing securities at compound interest, but the potential collapse of the debt pyramid (see Chapter 8 below) suggests this would be an unwise course in the long term.

DIAGRAM 4-1: RELATIVE CHANGES IN THE PURCHASING POWER OF $10.00 FEDERAL RESERVE NOTE and $10.00 LIBERTY GOLD COIN, 1914 TO 1976:

FEDERAL RESERVE NOTE

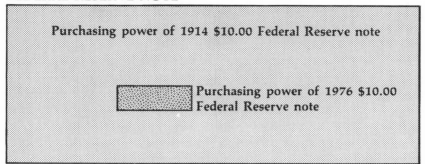

$10.00 LIBERTY GOLD COIN, 1914

*Bullion content 16.7 grams, with an approximate bullion value of $65.00 as of March 31, 1976.

estate, in silver dollars, while recording the transaction at the face value of the silver dollars for tax purposes.*

In brief, given the choice in 1914 — how to preserve $10 in wealth, in gold, silver, or paper — everything in history would counsel gold and silver, and gold and silver would have been the correct choice.

---

*I am not recommending this technique, but rather am commenting on the logical consequences of Internal Revenue Service policies. It is a subject that seems worth further investigation.

CHAPTER FIVE

The Paper Factory

> PATMAN: *How did you get the money to buy those two-billion dollars worth of government securities in 1933?*
>
> ECCLES: *We created it.*
>
> PATMAN: *Out of what?*
>
> ECCLES: *Out of the right to issue credit money.*
>
> PATMAN: *And there is nothing behind it, is there, except our Government's credit?*
>
> ECCLES: *That is what our money system is. If there were no debts in our money system, there wouldn't be any money.*
>
> Congressman Wright Patman questions Marriner Eccles, Governor of the Federal Reserve Board, (September 30, 1941, House Committee on Banking and Currency).

IF WE DO NOT HAVE A MONEY SYSTEM based on gold, with the option to take $10 gold Liberties for our pay check, then what kind of money system do we have? It might, without exaggeration, be called a paper factory or a debt machine.

Federal Reserve Board Governor Eccles' statement, "If there were no debts in our money system, there wouldn't be any money," puts the American money system, and the necessity for the war on gold, in a nutshell. Our money system, and almost all money systems in the modern world, are based on debt. One person's paper money or book-entry credit is another person's obligation to pay. The system is predicated on the heroic assumption that people will continue to accept another person's debts as an acceptable recompense.

But if a sizeable number of these debt-money holders decide they *don't* want the risk of taking someone else's promise to pay as a value in payment, what then? Suppose debt-money holders decide they would rather have more tangible assets than paper IOU's created out of nothing by the Federal Reserve System? For example, a paper mortgage has some tangible value because it is a legal claim on property, although it is itself an IOU and is part of the shaky debt pyramid. (See Chapter Eight.) Physical objects (houses, automobiles, cattle, even a keg of nails) are more tangible, and one day may be more marketable, than anonymous and untraceable paper promises. As we have seen, gold and silver are the ultimate tangible assets, and because of this universal acceptance even the anti-gold U.S. Treasury dares not dispose of its gold holdings *in toto*.

What then keeps the Federal Reserve System, which is based on paper debt, in operation? In one word, confidence. The confidence that someone else will accept a worthless piece of paper, created out of nothing and backed by nothing, in exchange for *their* real tangible objects. If confidence in this exchange erodes, then the rush is on. People will dump the paper fiat money or debt in exchange for tangible goods — *any* tangible goods with value. As the dumping process continues, usually fueled by rapid price increases, paper holders get less and less choosy about the type of real assets they will accept in exchange for paper. As Gresham's Law states, "Bad money (in this case, intangible paper) drives out good money (tangibles such as gold and silver)." In one sense, the assertion promoted by the anti-gold brigade that gold "is just another commodity" is accurate, because at some point the choice is always between paper fiat money and *any* commodities, of which gold and silver historically have been the preferred.

So the debt money system is a gigantic con game. The Eccles' principle, "If there were no debts in our money system, there wouldn't be any money," is founded on the assumption that citizens will always be willing to accept another person's liabilities for their own valuable goods. When confidence in the value of this inequitable exchange erodes, the end approaches; at least the end of that particular fiat money system. The Eccles debt-money Federal Reserve System is a paper money factory pyramided on a small base of real tangible gold reserves. Foreign exchange assets cannot be included in this tangible base, because with rare exceptions other countries have *their own* debt-money system. Thus, the only non-debt base for the paper pyramid is existing gold and silver reserves.

How did such a potentially disasterous system come to replace the stable gold standard in the United States? Let us now consider how the system arose and the amount of created debt which we know as money that is now poised on a minute gold base.

Jekyl Island: Creation of a Paper Mill

The Federal Reserve System is a legal private monopoly of the U.S. monetary system. Governmental influence is minimal; not even a General Accounting Office audit of the books is permissable. The Federal Reserve System has absolute power to issue notes and create credit and to do this for its own private profit, without accounting to Congress or anyone else. It is quite a remarkable system — the monopoly to end all monopolies!

How did this magnificent banking cornucopia ever receive the sanction of Congressional approval, and how does the Federal Reserve System evade investigation and audit? Oddly enough, very few factual studies have been made of the pressures and power plays that brought the system in to being and which have carefully protected the system from public probes.*

We do know this much: the Federal Reserve System is the brainchild of a single man, German banker Paul Warburg, who apparently was determined to share the "benefits" of central banking and fiat-note issues with the United States.

---

*For a quick review of the basic data, see: Gary Allen, *None Dare Call It Conspiracy*, (Seal Beach: Concord Press, 1971). Two other small investigative books worth examining are: Eustace Mullins, *The Federal Reserve Conspiracy*, (New Jersey: Christian Educational Association, 1954), and H. S. Kenan, *The Federal Reserve Bank*, (Los Angeles: Noontide Press, 1966).

Although the Federal Reserve System differs superficially from the European practice of central banks (there are twelve Federal Reserve districts, for example) the system is modelled on the German Reichsbank principle — and we have already described the results in 1923 of *that* principle.

The financial panic of 1907 was used by Congress as an excuse to form a National Monetary Commission. For two years this Commission roamed Europe studying European banking, at a cost to American taxpayers of $300,000. Out of this junket came a series of studies which promoted the concept of a private central bank for the United States.

The groundwork for the Federal Reserve System was laid at an unpublicized meeting at the J. P. Morgan Country Club on Jekyl Island, Georgia in November 1910. Senator Nelson Aldrich, bankers Frank Vanderlip (president of National City Bank and representing Rockefeller and Kuhn Loeb interests), Henry P. Davison (senior partner of J. P. Morgan), and Charles D. Norton (president of Morgan's First National Bank), met in secret to decide how to foist a central bank system on the United States. Others at the meeting were Paul Moritz Warburg, the German banker, and Benjamin Strong (a Morgan banker who later became first Governor of the Federal Reserve Bank of New York).

Out of the Jekyl Island cabal came the basic bill passed by Congress and signed into law by President Woodrow Wilson as the Federal Reserve Act of 1913. Under the earlier sub-Treasury system, bankers had no control over the money supply in the United States and, even less to their liking, none over currency issues.

In his autobiography, *From Farmboy to Financier*, Jekyl Island participant Frank Vanderlip was quite open about the origins of the Federal Reserve System:

> *Our secret expedition to Jekyl Island was the occasion of the actual conception of what eventually became the Federal Reserve System. The essential points of the Aldrich Plan were all contained in the Federal Reserve Act as it was passed.*

What does this Federal Reserve System do? The system creates money. It does so both as currency (Federal Reserve notes) and through its ability to influence the level of bank reserves, by creation of bank credit. The great virtue of this system, as seen through the eyes of the Fed itself, is that it provides "elasticity." Six decades of this "elasticity," the Fed claims, have produced growth in the economic system. FRS apologists compare this to pre-1913 when, it is argued, the money system could not grow because of an "inelastic currency." The latter assertion is subject to considerable disagreement, but, more importantly, the cost of an elastic currency has been depreciation of money and a monumental debt structure that is now in danger of collapse. In fact, the arguments put forward by the Federal Reserve System in favor of its operation do not differ from arguments put forward for other debt-creation schemes several centuries ago.*

In addition to a monopoly over the money system, the Federal Reserve exerts influence through the "revolving door" of New York-Washington appointments. Officials of the FRS frequently are appointed to the executive branch in Washington. Having determined U.S. policy, they then return to New York to reap the benefits.

The system, however, does not always produce lockstep action on the part of its appointees. It is true that one of the bitterest critics of gold has been Paul Volcker, formerly of Chase Manhattan Bank, one-time Deputy Secretary of the Treasury, and now president of the Federal Reserve Bank of New York. But by contrast, a contemporary pro-gold voice warning of the impending collapse of the debt pyramid is John Exter, former head of gold and silver operations for and vice president of the same Federal Reserve Bank of New York. Exter was also senior vice president of the First National City Bank.

The Supreme Role of Confidence

That the Federal Reserve System has worked at all is due to a single fact: the American public has believed in it. And until recently, in the absence of the full story of the formation and development of the Federal Reserve System, there was no reason why the public should lack confidence.

Public confidence is *always* the essential ingredient that

---

*See, Federal Reserve System, *The Federal Reserve System: Purposes and Functions*, (Washington D.C.: 1954).

keeps a fiat paper money or credit system operating. Without the confidence of the debt holders, the paper factory falls to the ground. Confidence in turn requires the maintenance of the belief that the store-of-wealth aspect of paper money or bank deposits will purchase what is needed, when it is needed. In other words, that the system is credit-worthy. In his 1828 classic, *Paper Against Gold*, William Cobbett recognized this intangible prerequisite:

> Credit *is a thing wholly dependent upon* opinion. *The word itself indeed has the same meaning as the word* belief. *As long as men* believe *in the riches of any individual, or any company, so long he or they possess all the advantages of riches. But when once* suspicion *is excited, no matter from what cause, the* credit *is shaken: and a very little matter oversets it.* *

Cobbett's emphasis on the intangible of "opinion" or "belief" is confirmed by Pelatiah Webster, an early Philadelphia businessman who wrote in 1780 on the ill-advised enforcement of fiat money by the Pennsylvania Assembly and the issue of the Continental currency:

> *The thing which makes money an object of desire — which gives it strength of motive on the hearts of all men — is the general confidence, the opinion which it gains as a sovereign means of obtaining everything needful. This confidence, this opinion, exists in the mind only, and is not compellable or assailable by force, but must be grounded on that evidence and reason which the mind can see and believe.* †

We can cite parallel views from the Federal Reserve System itself, at least in the words of John Exter:

> *Paper money expansionism will not work . . . [but] even highly sophisticated monetary authorities go on for years accepting ever more worthless paper instead of*

---

*William Cobbett, *Paper Against Gold* (London: W. M. Cobbett, 1828).

†*Strictures on Tender Acts*, (reprinted as *Not Worth a Continental*) (Irvington on Hudson: The Foundation for Economic Education Inc., 1950), p. 12.

demanding gold. . . . But the time has come at last when people, including even foreign central bankers, no longer want to hold more and more and ever more worthless currencies. . . . Confidence in a currency can erode rapidly once it becomes inconvertible, for only convertibility enables it to maintain its store of value function indefinitely. . . . Without convertibility, history shows that a currency will ultimately become worthless and disappear.*

It is agreed then that the essential factor required for a workable fiat money-credit system is the factor of *confidence*. As John Exter stated explicitly in 1976, and Pelatiah Webster implicitly in 1780, it is gold, a relatively scarce but measurable and identifiable substance, that has the ability to maintain confidence in the value of a money. Gold is scarce, therefore money cannot be generated by whim. Paper is plentiful, and thus can easily be generated. Once the public believes that paper money is generated by whim, without any real value, then such "money" is no longer acceptable as a store of value. It will continue to circulate for a while, buying less and less goods for more and more paper. When confidence is shaken — and historically convertibility into gold is the acid test of confidence — then a run starts to convert paper into gold or other tangible assets, and the paper soon depreciates to zero. Paper can indeed serve temporarily as a store of value. But as paper only *represents* a store of value, it is a fragile, easily abused storage system; the holder of paper proxies is instinctively wary that printing-paper debt has not created stores of value, but rather is an artiface to be distrusted.

Consequently, confidence is the single attribute that the operator of a paper money or credit system must maintain at all costs. Yet the modern United States paper factory since 1971 has produced not only inconvertible paper money, but seemingly has little understanding that the system will collapse once confidence in this paper is shaken. Even the inscriptions on Federal Reserve notes taunt the bearer. The notes progressively reduced the prom-

---

*"Gold: The international means of payment" in G. C. Wiegand (Ed.), *Inflation and Monetary Crisis*, (Washington, D.C.: Public Affairs Press, 1975), p. 143.

ise to pay or convert into gold or silver, until by 1975 there is no promise to pay the holder anything.

The 1928 series gold certificate included the following inscription:

> *THIS CERTIFIES THAT THERE HAVE BEEN DEPOSITED IN THE TREASURY OF THE UNITED STATES OF AMERICA, TEN DOLLARS IN GOLD COIN PAYABLE TO THE BEARER ON DEMAND.*

This is a straightforward and understandable commitment by the note issuer. If the holder of this $10.00 bill goes to the Treasury he can obtain ten dollars worth of gold coin in exchange. So long as the holder has confidence in the specie reserves of the U.S. Treasury, there is little chance the paper bill-gold coin exchange will be requested. But if confidence is shattered, then demands for exchange will be prompt — there will be a "run on the bank" demanding gold. Under a fractional reserve system, gold reserves are only a fraction of the outstanding "gold certificates;" even in 1928 the Treasury could not have met all demands for payment had such a run started.

The 1928 series Federal Reserve note made a commitment identical to the gold certificate:

> *THE UNITED STATES OF AMERICA WILL PAY TO THE BEARER ON DEMAND TEN DOLLARS. REDEEMABLE IN GOLD ON DEMAND AT THE UNITED STATES TREASURY.*

The Federal Reserve note of 1928 was "as good as gold." It found acceptability as readily as $10 in gold coin, and would continue to do so as long as the note holders believed in the promise of convertibility on demand.

The 1934 Series silver certificates promised to pay in silver, rather than gold:

> *THIS CERTIFIES THAT THERE IS ON DEPOSIT IN THE TREASURY OF THE UNITED STATES OF AMERICA TEN DOLLARS IN SILVER PAYABLE TO THE BEARER ON DEMAND.*

The pledge on the silver certificate was even stronger; it promised not only complete convertibility, but also that sufficient specie in silver to redeem *all* outstanding certificates was on deposit with the U.S. Treasury.

In 1934, the use of weasel words to deceive the American public about their currency began, when Franklin D. Roosevelt rejected convertibility of bank notes into gold. The 1934 Series of Federal Reserve notes was changed to read:

THE UNITED STATES OF AMERICA WILL PAY TO THE BEARER ON DEMAND TEN DOLLARS. REDEEMABLE IN LAWFUL MONEY AT THE UNITED STATES TREASURY.

This inscription was repeated on the Series 1950 Federal Reserve notes. Note that there is nothing about redemption in gold or silver — just a promise to pay in "lawful money." From time to time citizens sent these bills to the U.S. Treasury asking for exchange in "lawful money." In reply, the Treasury merely sent other Federal Reserve notes, of equal value and bearing the same inscriptions. In other words, all one piece of green paper is worth is another piece of green paper. (No doubt some of these curious citizens reflected about the changes in their currency, and the replies they received from the Treasury; if they did, they probably became gold bugs.)

In 1963 the Treasury decided to do away with the nonsense of exchanging pieces of paper for other pieces of paper. The 1963 Series of Federal Reserve notes merely states:

THIS NOTE IS LEGAL TENDER FOR ALL DEBTS PUBLIC OR PRIVATE.

The Federal Reserve note of 1975 is simply a piece of paper with silk threads woven in it, printed with green and black ink. Intrinsically it is no different from billions of other pieces of paper that might be printed. Changes in the "promise to pay" inscription during the past several decades reflect a declining appreciation of the requirement for conversion into gold or silver.

So what does the holder of a current Federal Reserve note actually command? He holds a piece of rectangular paper of no intrinsic value, worth a fraction of a cent as waste paper. And that is all! To be sure, the vast majority of note holders *assume* they hold something more valuable than a fancy piece of green-and-black printed paper. Reality's grim explosion has yet to occur. But when it comes — when confidence is broken — belief in those pieces of paper as representing wealth will be broken and the rush will be on to turn paper into goods, any goods.

Nobel Prize-winning economist Milton Friedman has described the circular thinking which underlies the system in the following words:

> . . . *each accepts them [the pieces of paper] because he is confident others will. The pieces of green paper have value because everybody thinks they have value, and everybody thinks they have value because in his experience they have had value.* *

In the final analysis, emphasizes Friedman, acceptance of paper "is a social convention which owes its very existence to the mutual acceptance of what from one point of view is a fiction." †

Assault on the Paper Factory

This fiction that value is inherent in rectangular pieces of paper is an irritant to some American citizens, who go to great lengths to challenge the paper factory. Their professed goal is to bring down the walls so that fiction money can be replaced with substantive money.

In recent years the United States has been dotted with individual pinprick assaults on the paper factory system. Such challenges may seem to be futile, for they have done little to damage the acceptability of Federal Reserve notes. But such a view would be shortsighted; in the longer run such attacks are early warning signals. A few individuals are following a centuries-old pattern of rejection of fiat money and reversion to hard money. In Bunker Hill, Illinois in 1973, for example, Rev. Casimir F. Gierut claimed in court that the Federal Reserve System has no constitutional authority to issue money. Although the Fed was created by Congress, Rev. Gierut argued that the system is unlawful be-

---

*Milton Friedman and Anna Schwartz, *A Monetary History of the United States, 1867-1960*, (Princeton: Princeton University Press, 1963), p. 696.
† *Ibid.*

cause the notes are issued by the Federal Reserve System, but signed by the Treasurer and Secretary of the Treasury. Rev. Gierut demanded that the Secret Service arrest the entire Board of Governors of the Federal Reserve System on the grounds that "they are the greatest ring of counterfeiters you've ever seen."*

Other challenges on Constitutional grounds have been waged against the legality of the Federal Reserve note. William Dobslaw of South Bend, Indiana refused a check from the Mishiwaka Redevelopment Department, as payment for a building scheduled for demolition, on the grounds it was not money as defined in the Constitution: "Since today's Federal Reserve notes are irredeemable in anything except paper," Dobslaw claimed, they are illegal.

In Fresno, California, James W. Scott sought dismissal of charges that he failed to file income tax returns in 1969 and 1970 on the grounds that he was paid in worthless Federal Reserve notes; therefore he had received no income, therefore he owed no Federal tax. The District Judge didn't quite see it the same way — Article I, Section 10 of the Constitution notwithstanding — and ruled against Scott.

Another Indiana case based on Article I, Section 10 of the Constitution was heard in 1974. Dr. O. Walter Calvin, a South Bend physician, refused to accept a State of Indiana check for $74 in payment for treatment of an employee of the State Highway Department. Dr. Calvin demanded gold or silver in payment, as prescribed in the Constitution. Judge John L. Niblack didn't agree and ruled that the Constitution gave the Congress exclusive right to say what is legal tender; besides, the State of Indiana had no gold or silver to pay Dr. Calvin.

It is perhaps understandable that the jurist would be reluctant to declare his own pay check unconstitutional. But how he decided the Constitution gave Congress the right to decide what is legal tender, when the document itself says something quite different, is somewhat puzzling. Only in one case have these pinprick assaults on the paper factory received a favorable court decision. The nature of the argument used by the court makes that case a story in itself.

Coin World, May 30, 1973.

Court Declares Federal Notes Worthless

In December 1968 Judge Martin V. Mahoney handed down a decision in which he declared Federal Reserve notes to be invalid. Moreover, the First National Bank of Montgomery — which stood to lose $14,000 — did not appeal the decision. The bank apparently preferred to lose $14,000 (or was instructed to lose the money), rather than appeal the issue to a higher court. The reluctance to appeal almost guarantees that at some future date a well-financed and researched legal attack on the paper factory will be made on similar grounds.

In 1967, the First National Bank of Montgomery, Minnesota began legal proceedings to foreclose on a mortgage held by Jerome Daly and secured by property at Fairview Beach, Scott County, Minnesota. After following due procedures the bank went to court to acquire possession of the property in an action before Scott County Justice of the Peace Martin V. Mahoney. In his presentation to the jury, defendent Daly made a simple point: the bank had no right to the property because it did not, when advancing funds for the mortgage, give him anything of real value upon which to base a claim for the property. The $14,000 was not specie or even "legal tender;" it was simply a bookkeeping entry. The bank argued that this was standard practice, but did not cite a statute authorizing it to create such credit by a bookkeeping entry.

Justice Mahoney rendered the following decision:

> The issues in this case were simple. There was no material dispute on the facts for the jury to resolve. Plaintiff admitted that it, in combination with the Federal Reserve Bank of Minneapolis, which are for all practical purposes, because of their interlocking activity and practices, and both being Banking Institutions Incorporated under the Laws of the United States, are in the Law to be treated as one and same Bank, did create the entire $14,000 in money or credit upon its books by bookkeeping entry. That this was the Consideration used to support the Note dated May 8, 1964, and the Mortgage of the same date. The money and credit first came into existence when they created it. Mr. Morgan (for the Bank) admitted that no United States Law or

*Statute existed which gave him the right to do this. A
lawful consideration must exist and be tendered to support the Note. See Anheuser-Busch Brewing Co., v.
Emma Mason, 44 Minn. 318, 46 N.W. 558. The Jury
found there was no lawful consideration and I agree.
Only God can create something of value out of nothing.*

*Even if Defendent could be charged with waiver or
estoppel as a matter of Law this is no defense to the
Plaintiff. The law leaves wrongdoers where it finds
them. See sections 50, 51, and 52 of Am Jur 2d "Actions" on page 584 — "no claim based upon, or in any
manner depending upon, a fraudulent, illegal, or im-
moral transaction or contract to which Plaintiff was party."*

*No complaint was made by Plaintiff that Plaintiff
did not receive a fair trial. From the admissions made by
Mr. Morgan the path of duty was made clear for the
Jury. Their verdict could not reasonably have been
otherwise. Justice was rendered completely and without
delay, freely and without purchase, conformable to the
laws in this Court on December 7, 1968.*

By the Court.

/s/ Martin V. Mahoney.

The bank appealed this decision and tendered $2.00 to the
clerk of the court as fees. The notes tendered by the bank's attor-
ney were a one-dollar bill issued by the Federal Reserve Bank of
San Francisco (No. L1278283C) and a one-dollar bill issued by the
Federal Reserve Bank of Minnesota (No. 180410697A). Justice
Mahoney refused to accept these Federal Reserve notes and cited
Article 1, Section 10 of the Constitution: "No State shall make
any Thing but gold and silver coin a tender in payment of debts."
The two dollar bills tendered were not in fact "dollars," but
worthless pieces of paper, according to the Judge.

Rather than appeal to higher court, the First National Bank
of Montgomery abandoned its $14,000 and claim to the pro-
perty. Obviously prudence was the better part of valor for these
bankers. Apparently it chose not to run any risk that might have
put itself (and 5,000 other banks) out of business.

The legality of Federal Reserve notes and creation of credit by the Federal Reserve System still have to face a full legal and constitutional challenge. A low-level court ruling is not binding in other cases or even recognized by other courts. A higher court test of this fundamental issue would be interesting indeed.

The latest decision at time of going to press (1977) was a decision of the Ninth Circuit Court of Appeals in San Francisco dated April 1, 1976 (*U.S. vs. Wangrud*). This case was on appeal from the U.S. District Court where Wangrud argued that he had not found it necessary to file a Federal Income Tax return because his pay checks could only be cashed for Federal Reserve notes — and these are not redeemable in specie. The Court of Appeals rejected this interpretation and upheld the District Court: we ". . . make it clear that this argument has absolutely no merit. We affirm this conviction."

The conflict represented by these legal challenges is a conflict between the power of the Government to decree what is legal tender and the natural right of people to determine what they will accept as money. This conflict has been expressed by Arthur Kemp in these words:

> *All our money became full legal tender in 1933. This means only that all our money is equally good, in statute law, so far as making payments is concerned. It can also be said, with accuracy, that all our money is equally bad. It is not true, and it is difficult to see why anyone should have thought that it could be true, that all our money is equally good, or usable, so far as service as reserves against note issue and deposits is concerned.*
>
> *What we have in practice, of course, is a system based upon promises to pay dollars with virtually no mechanism for insuring the continuity or stability of the basic monetary unit. Although we have most of the attributes that can be considered the essence of an inconvertible and irredeemable paper money standard, we still retain the semi-fiction that paper money is a promise to pay at some indefinite time, or if one prefers, on demand. The latter is technically correct. In fact, however, failure to pay or the impossibility of paying makes the former more accurate. Had the purposes of the legal qualities of money not been disregarded, we would have*

*at least been faced with the necessity of saying of a piece of paper: "This IS a dollar."**

This trickle of assaults on the paper factory is of greater long-run consequence than the U.S. Treasury and Congress may appreciate. These cases represent the surfacing of doubts about the stability of the fiction known as the U.S. dollar. They are based on grassroots suspicion (or conviction!) that our present fiat currency does not offer a store of value and therefore does not constitute acceptable money. True, Congress has passed laws making Federal Reserve notes legal tender, as the Court of Appeals states in *U.S. vs. Wangrud*. It can pass many more, saying the same thing in stronger terms. However, there is nothing Congress can do, short of shutting down the U.S. economy, to make people accept Federal Reserve notes as money when they decide not to do so. It is this most important distinction, identified by Talleyrand 200 years ago, that is once again making its presence felt.

People — at least a few people, so far — are saying, "This is *not* a dollar." Are they voices crying in a wilderness who will be neither heeded nor remembered? Or the first few harbingers of a mighty storm that will soon be upon us?

History suggests the latter. And, having arrived at this point, it is now time to look at the war on gold itself.

---

*Arthur Kemp, *The Legal Qualities of Money*, (New York: Pageant Press, New York, nd), p. 11.

PART TWO
GOLD VERSUS PAPER

CHAPTER SIX

The War of the Gold Pool

> Said the Crawling Peg
> To the Dirty Float
> "We're two lost souls
> In a leaky boat,
> And down below there's a hole in the hold
> That can't be plugged with Paper Gold."

With acknowledgements to John Chamberlain, *Freeman*, April 1974.

AT THE END OF WORLD WAR II the United States was in a unique and seemingly unassailable monetary position. The world's largest gold stock was secure in the vaults of Fort Knox and the Federal Reserve Banks. The American dollar was everywhere in short supply, facing an apparently insatiable demand. American technology and the standard of living it made possible were the envy of the world.

Three decades later the United States is wracked by internal political and moral problems, inflation, and self doubts. The world's most powerful nation had been defeated by a third-rate country in a wasteful no-win war. Half of its gold stock had been lost, and it had short-term liabilities to foreigners totalling almost ten times the value of what gold it still owned.

What happened, and why?

In the late 1950s astute European financial observers brought certain unfavorable monetary signals to the attention of their respective governments. In January 1959 Jacques Rueff, a well-known French economist, sent a memorandum to the French Finance Minister, pointing out that while the franc might be convertible into dollars, under the Bretton Woods agreement only the dollar could be converted into gold. This meant, Rueff added, that the operation of the gold exchange standard and the American deficit made it increasingly unlikely that the dollar, and thus the franc, would continue to be converted into gold. Subsequently, three articles in *Le Monde* on the 27th, 28th, and 29th of June 1961 carried Rueff's ominous message to the general reader.*

In these articles, written, it should be noted, in 1961, Rueff warned that the gold exchange standard was a "danger to the West." Because of its linkage with the U.S. dollar, day by day the Free World was being brought closer to the brink of another Great Depression. Rueff pointed to the danger posed by Resolution 9 of the 1922 Genoa International Monetary Conference, which attempted to practice economy in the use of gold "by maintaining reserves in the form of foreign balances." Such a system, using foreign balances as assets for reserve purposes, enabled national banks of issue to create money, not only on the basis of their gold stock as was customary, but also on foreign exchange payable in gold. (Sterling and dollars after World War I; dollars alone after Bretton Woods in 1944.)

Under a pure gold standard (as contrasted to a gold exchange standard), any influx of dollars into post-war Europe would have required counter-balancing payments in gold. But under the gold exchange standard which was in effect in 1944 the dollars remained on deposit at the American point of origin and were loaned out again to domestic borrowers. Between 1951 and the end of December 1961 the United States thus accumulated a total deficit of $18 billion on its balance of payments. The consequences of these deficits were not perceived by the Keynesian-oriented economists running the show, who see the U.S. as a closed economic system in which balance of payments deficits can be ignored.

Under a pure gold standard the gold stock in the U.S. would

---

*Reprinted in other periodicals, including the *Times* of London and *Fortune* in the United States.

have declined by this amount to offset foreign claims; in short, a deficit would have induced an equivalent export of gold. But in actual practice, from 1950 to 1960 the U.S. gold stock declined by only 23 percent, or $5.3 billion (from $22.8 to $17.5 billion). These accumulated American deficits had been settled not by gold shipments but in paper dollars. European creditor banks had promptly reinvested about two-thirds of these paper dollars back in the United States. In this way, between 1951 and 1961 foreign banks of issue had increased their foreign dollar holdings by about $13 billion.

In brief, about one-third of the U.S. balance of payments deficit in the 1950s had been settled in gold and the other two-thirds were settled — "just as if the deficit had not existed" — by printing money. Rueff phrased the American problem more caustically:

> *In this way, the gold-exchange standard brought about an immense revolution and produced the secret of a deficit without tears. It allowed the countries in possession of a currency benefiting from international prestige to give without taking, to lend without borrowing, and to acquire without paying.**

Rueff suggested that this "revolution" was not a deliberate policy on the part of the United States but was in fact a "collective error." But he added: "when people became aware of it, [it] will be viewed by history as an object of astonishment and scandal."

Perhaps Rueff was correct and the deficits were not a deliberate objective of U.S. policy. Even so, it must be recognized that the United States did nothing to solve the problem after it was identified. Long after the danger was noted and recorded in the academic literature, the United States in the 60s and 70s continued with policies of acquiring something for nothing; the policy makers continued to act as though there was an international "free lunch" available for the taking, without a day of reckoning.

It was not an American but a French economist, Jacques Rueff, who in a series of books and articles attempted to draw

---

*J. Rueff, *The Monetary Sin of the West*, (New York: MacMillan, 1972), p. 23.

world attention to the dangers of an inconvertible dollar. Most American economists, and certainly all those of note, were busy devising face-saving algebraic equations or encouraging further deficits by planning expenditures of the vast dollar flow. Let us then look more closely at the nature of the monetary problem facing the United States in the late 1950s.

The Critical Crossover in 1959

The overseas financial crisis facing the United States in 1959 could be easily read from the monetary statistics. Indeed, it could hardly be overlooked by economists whose job it is to analyze and advise on international monetary affairs. The crisis identified by Rueff was certainly known; the trouble was that no economist in the United States wanted to face the issue, or more probably face the ire of the politicians who would have to be told they were spending the U.S. into a catastrophe.

Chart 6-1 and Table 6-1 present United States external liquid liabilities on an annual basis, compared to the United States gold stock, between 1950 and the early 1970s. Before 1950 the U.S. gold stock was comfortably larger than the aggregate amounts owed to all international lending institutions, private foreigners, and monetary authorities combined. A decade later, in 1959, the curve of external liquid liabilities had crossed over the amount of the gold stock valued at the official price; by the end of the 1960s overseas liabilities were three to four times greater than the gold stock. By 1973 external liabilities totaled more or less $100 billion (depending on what one included) and the gold stock was worth a mere $10 billion. In 1973, liabilities were ten times greater than the gold stock. The United States was technically bankrupt. If called upon to meet its overseas liabilities in gold it could not do so.

Two basic choices were available at the crossover point in 1959: either (1) repudiate gold or (2) abandon the "official price" for gold and allow an upvaluation in the market place to bring U.S. external liabilities and its revalued gold stock closer in line. The United States chose to repudiate its promises to pay foreign claims in gold. Since that time it has attempted to eliminate gold from the international monetary scene.

CHART 6-1: U.S. GOLD AND FOREIGN DOLLAR HOLDINGS, 1949-1959 (BILLIONS OF DOLLARS)

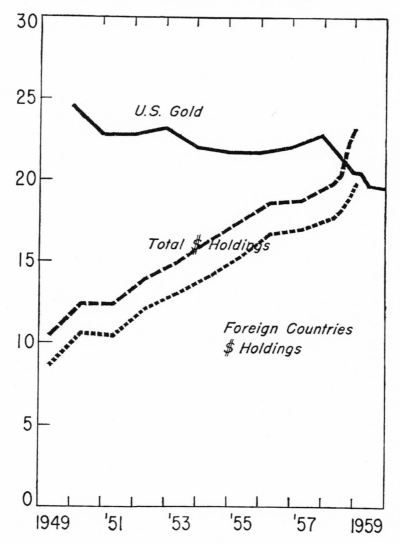

Source: Robert Triffin, *Gold and the Dollar Crisis, The Future of Convertibility*, (New Haven: Yale University Press, 1960).

TABLE 6-1: U.S. SHORT-TERM LIABILITIES TO FOREIGNERS AND THE GOLD STOCK, 1955-1971 (in $ millions).

Year	Short Term Liabilities to Foreigners	Gold Stock @ $35/oz	@ $150/oz
1955	$11,895	$21,753	$93,227
1960	$18,701	$17,804	$76,303
1965	$25,551	$13,806	$59,168
1968	$31,717	$10,892	$46,680
1971	$55,417	$10,206	$43,740
1974	$95,000	$11,830	$50,700

Source: U.S. Department of Commerce Publication, *Statistical Abstract of the United States, 1975*, (Washington, D.C., Bureau of the Census, 1975), and International Monetary Fund, *International Financial Statistics, December 1975*, (Washington, D.C.: December 1975), Volume XXVIII, Number 12.

Treasury advisers surely knew that such a policy had never succeeded in all the centuries that man had used gold as a medium of exchange. These advisers included some of the better known (and better paid) academic economists who present themselves in graduate seminars as living oracles of historical wisdom; yet history records (as we noted in Chapter Two) that a war on gold has never succeeded.

The alternate policy available to the Washington policymakers was to abandon the "official price" of gold and allow the market place to reflect the suppressed market forces of the previous several decades. There was general agreement in 1960, even among bitter opponents of gold, that market forces would reflect a substantially higher gold price. Such a higher price for gold would have enabled the United States to avoid the monetary crisis of the 60s and the devaluation crises of the 70s, by bringing upvalued reserves into line with liabilities.

The monetary statistics tell the story. In 1955 U.S. short-term foreign liabilities were $11.9 billion and its gold stock (valued at the official $35 an ounce) was worth $21.7 billion. In other words, short-term liabilities were covered 1.8 times by the gold stock at the official price. However, if the market valued gold at $150 an ounce, then the U.S. stock was worth over $93 billion, and covered overseas liabilities 7.8 times. In brief, there was no problem in 1955 if (a) the U.S. had taken steps to meet its persistent deficits on balance of payments, or (b) allowed the market to set the gold price and establish a healthy coverage for foreign liabilities.

The United States instead chose to do nothing. By 1960 the dilemma was painfully obvious. On the chart the curve of short-term liabilities ($18.7 billion) had crossed over the gold stock valued at $35/oz. ($17.8 billion). Gold coverage was now only .95, instead of 1.8 as in 1955. At $150 an ounce liabilities were still covered four times, so the option yet remained of allowing an upward revaluation of gold to help solve the deficit problem. There was still time to act, but it was running out.

By 1968 the position had worsened; at $35 an ounce the U.S. had only .34 coverage; at $150 an ounce coverage was 1.47 times liabilities. Just three years later, in 1971, even at $150 an ounce coverage of overseas liabilities was only .79, and at the official price of $35/oz. it was a mere .18 times. By 1974 the coverage had deteriorated even further: .12 at $35/oz. and .53 at $150/oz.

How did our American monetary experts react to Rueff's warning and the available statistics? Some years earlier, Robert Triffin, one of the few Americans who recognized the brewing crisis, discussed the dollar-gold predicament in his book, *Europe and the Money Muddle*.* With the worsening statistics on overseas dollar deficits in mind, Triffin wrote: "It is evident that such a movement could not continue indefinitely without eventually undermining confidence in the dollar itself." But when Triffin considered possible solutions, he immediately dismissed a return to a pure gold standard. Why an out-of-hand rejection of this solution? Because a gold standard, in Triffin's words, "gravely endangers the continued expansion of production and international trade." This question of international liquidity has already been rejected as irrelevent. Triffin commented that periodically the South African delegation to the annual meetings of the International Monetary Fund suggested upward revaluation of gold in terms of dollars and other currencies as the solution. He agrees this solution would work, but refuses to consider it. Why? Because, says Triffin,

---

*Robert Triffin, (New Haven: Yale University Press, 1957), p. 297.

> *Such a revaluation ... would have to be very*
> *drastic indeed to meet the dimensions of the problem*
> *suggested ... and would appear totally unpalatable to*
> *public opinion in the United States and many other*
> *countries.* *

Such a revaluation would certainly have to be "very drastic indeed," because the official depression of gold — $35 to $42 an ounce since 1934 — had been "very drastic indeed." One cannot cite artificial official maneuvers with the gold price in the past as a logical reason for rejection of the market solution now. Arguing that such a revaluation would be "unpalatable to public opinion" is really a euphemism for the opinion of Triffin and other experts. The public knows little about the intricacies of international finance, and has little concern about the price of gold *per se*. It is more to the point that revaluation would demonstrate the inherent weaknesses of the "paper factory" (see Chapter Five), to the dismay of a significant proportion of our Keynesian-bred "experts." Revaluation would be "unpalatable" because it would demonstrate that monetary experts had no historical grasp or appreciation of the role of money as a store of value. As Ludwig von Mises remarked in a comment recorded earlier,† these inflationists "do not care a whit for the future of their nation and its civilization."

Similarly, Walter Gardner of the International Monetary Fund staff rejected the concept of "marking up" the price of gold because it would set off a major anticipatory speculation. It probably would set off an upward move because, as we have already noted, the price of gold has been artificially depressed by government decrees; it would certainly go through a "catch-up" period. But is aesthetic dislike of speculative profit a valid reason arbitrarily to reject gold as a monetary medium, if it offers promise of a solution?

The crux of the problem is that Triffin and other experts really object to gold on ideological grounds. Triffin put it like this:

Ibid., p. 298.

† See p. 74.

> *Most of all, the barrenness of this proposal [i.e., to use gold] makes it most repugnant to those who think that the international need for liquidity can be put to better use than financing digging gold from the entrails of the earth and reburying it in the vaults of Fort Knox and other gold graves.* *

Repugnance is a value judgment. Triffin and the monetary experts are abhorred by mining gold. Yet others may have other value judgments. It is equally reasonable to argue that we should favor gold since tobacco-chewing gold miners are a more deserving group than jet-setting, meeting-hopping, international monetary experts. At least the gold miners work a lot harder and get us into far less trouble than the monetary experts.

The critical danger is that because of this ideological repugnance toward gold, U.S. overseas liabilities in 1970 were ten times or so in excess of U.S. gold stocks when valued at the official price. If the holders of these overseas claims called for payment *in gold* (and in part they did), the U.S. could not meet its debts. It is a useless self-serving policy, transparent to Europeans, to call for demonetization of gold. Does anyone in the Treasury believe that the Europeans will go along? The answer can be found in the records of European gold stocks. While the U.S. has been calling for the demonetization of gold, the European central bank gold reserve holdings have soared.

The War of the Gold Pool

The drain of gold from U.S. official reserves in the early 1960s did not go unnoticed among sharp-eyed traders who make their living by correcting other people's mistaken judgments. According to successive U.S. Treasury Secretaries, there is a breed of canny Swiss bankers, colloquially known as the "Gnomes of Zurich," who delight in tweaking Uncle Sam's nose at his expense and their profit. Of course, no one, not even justifiably renowned Swiss bankers, can make a profit unless a profit-making opportunity exists. Quite often, the act of attempting to take the profit automatically eliminates the profit opportunity. With

---

*Ibid., p. 299.

gold, Uncle Sam masochistically persisted in maintaining a profitable opportunity and then blamed the Swiss bankers for accepting the open invitation to clean up.

The exit of gold from the Federal Reserve vaults to European central banks in the 1960s, coupled with continuing balance of payments deficits, was a "sure-thing" signal to market
observers. Gold at $35 an ounce was underpriced. European
central banks were replenishing their reserves, so investors and
speculators — including, no doubt, many Swiss bankers — joined
the parade.

In 1960 gold on the London free market touched $40.60 an
ounce, an unusually high figure for the time. Distrust of paper
money surfaced in several countries — repeating the age-old historical lessons revealed by the French assignat, the Continental
bill, and countless other extinct currencies. More and more individuals began to buy gold as a more reliable store of wealth.

The official response to the upward move in the free market
was to sell gold to dampen the price rise. To do this, the London
Gold Pool was formed by the United States, United Kingdom,
France, West Germany, Switzerland, Italy, Belgium, and the
Netherlands, with the United States taking a one-half share of the
pool's operation. The function of the pool was to maintain the
"official price" of gold at $35 an ounce.

Herein lies a puzzle. Responsible Treasury officials are well-
educated, technically sophisticated individuals. Yet what these
officials tried to do in the 1967 Gold Pool operation could be torn
to shreds by any college freshman who took a one-semester
course in economics. Some 30 million Americans have reportedly
had the benefit of Economics 1A (the introductory economics
course) so we can present the Gold Pool operation in simple
diagrammatic supply-and-demand curves familiar to them.
Theoretically, the 1960 gold market looked something like the
diagram on page 109.

There was an aggregate demand for gold (D-D) from individuals and, as we have seen, from central banks. There was an
aggregate supply (S-S) from newly mined South African and
Russian gold, plus some selling by the Federal Reserve in the
United States, the United Kingdom, and perhaps a few other
minor sources. The market price reflected these aggregate forces
of supply and demand. The top London free market price in 1967

CHART 6-2: SUPPLY AND DEMAND FOR GOLD IN 1967.*

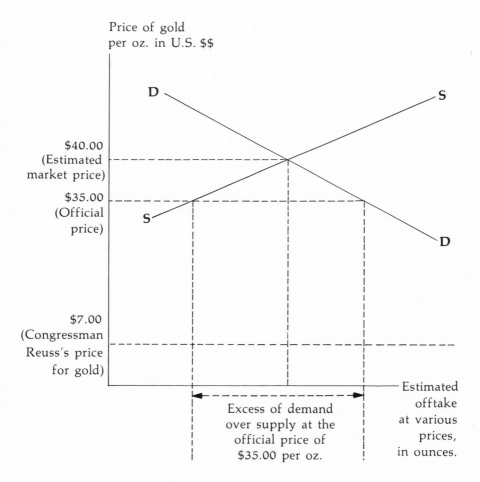

Price of gold
per oz. in U.S. $$

D   S

$40.00
(Estimated
market price)

$35.00
(Official
price)

S

D

$7.00
(Congressman
Reuss's price
for gold)

Excess of demand
over supply at the
official price of
$35.00 per oz.

Estimated
offtake
at various
prices,
in ounces.

* The supply curve for gold is unusual. Supply curves are always presented in textbooks as upward sloping to the right, as in Chart 6-2 above. However, new mine supplies of gold conform to a curve sloping downward to the right, like the demand curve. This phenomenen is not treated in textbooks. Mining practice is to use lower-ore grades (and thus reduce total gold output), as market price increases, in order to lengthen the life of the mine. The aggregate supply curve above is a composite of new mine supplies and dishoarding by central banks and individuals, but gives insufficient weighting to new mine supplies.

was $40 an ounce; in some places with government restrictions on gold holding (such as India), the local free market (black market) price was considerably above the London price. The London free market price in 1960 ranged up to $40/oz., while the official price was $35/oz.

What the London Gold Pool heroically set out to do, under the leadership of the United States with the Europeans glumly in tow, was to keep the gold price at $35/oz. by dumping gold onto the free market. Why $35/oz. no one bothered to explain. Why not $30, or $40, or even $50 an ounce? We don't know. The official price was $35 an ounce and apparently the Treasury believed, somewhat like King Canute, that if a Treasury edict would not stop the tide in the English channel, at least it could most certainly establish a price for a barbaric relic like gold. Jacques Rueff has suggested that it just never occurred to these Washington monetary experts that the U.S. balance of payments equilibrium could be restored through a gold policy, and that the "official price" policy was self-defeating.* We believe it probably *did* occur to these experts to use gold, but for ideological reasons they rejected such a solution for two reasons: first, a gold policy would challenge the supremacy of the paper dollar; and second, post-Keynesian policies have been built on an anti-gold policy to advance political internationalism. Keynes himself, while promoting a World Authority, was not as explicitly and vehemently anti-gold as many of his pupils. Keynes freely admitted in his *Treatise on Money*† that gold "has been fairly successful over longish periods in maintaining a reasonable stability of purchasing." This is an admission indeed from an economist who argued that Commodity Money (gold) has given way to Representative Money (paper). More to the point, Keynes also acknowledged that gold:

> . . . *keeps slovenly currency systems up to the mark. It limits the discretion and fetters the independent action of the Government or Central Bank of any country which has bound itself to the international gold standard.*‡

*J. Rueff, *op. cit.*, p. 117.
† J. M. Keynes, (London: Macmillan & Co., Ltd., 1960), Volume II, p. 293.
‡*Ibid.*, p. 229.

Keynes probably would have allowed time and tradition to work at the demonetization of gold, and might have advised against the outright war waged by the Keynesians at the Treasury.

In any event, in 1961 the United States and the European central banks formed the London Gold Pool as a market-stabilizing (that is, price-depressing) device. When the gold offtake into private hands raised the price, the pool sold gold. When the private offtake reversed and private sales drove the price below $35, the Gold Pool bought. As a result, the Gold Pool very quickly lost $991 million from the stocks of central banks in the United States, United Kingdom, France, Switzerland, Belgium, Italy, the Netherlands, and West Germany. Officially the blame for the drain was placed on the Gnomes of Zurich, but the real cause was simply that the official price was set well below the market clearing price (see Chart 6-2), with predictable results.

French economists and French Treasury officials maintained their inherent sense of logic, read the writing on the wall, and, in June 1967, withdrew from the Gold Pool rather than risk the loss of their own gold stocks. Even earlier, in August and September 1966, France had become a vigorous *buyer* of gold, outside the pool, to build up its reserves. Moreover, France took physical possession of its gold, rather than leave it in the vaults of the Federal Reserve Bank in New York.

In all, the United States lost $571 million of gold and France gained $601 million in 1966. When France withdrew from the pool the United States picked up her share of the operations, meaning the U.S. now had 59 percent of the pool rather than 50 percent.

Defeat turned to disaster between November 1967 and March 1968, as the U.S. lost a staggering $3.2 billion from its gold stocks. By this time other European central banks followed the French example and told the United States that further defense of the dollar would require U.S. gold; none of theirs would be available. The end came on March 14, 1968, the day the Gold Pool lost *400 tons* of gold to private buyers. The loss of 20 percent of the U.S. gold stocks within five months finally galvanized the Treasury into action. At the request of the Federal Reserve Bank and the U.S. Treasury, President Lyndon Johnson asked the Bank of England to close the Gold Pool operation.

Why didn't the London Gold Pool succeed? Economic logic is simple. The official price was well below the market clearing price, and thus established a massive leak as central bankers turned in their claims for "cheap" $35 gold. If the official price had been raised to the market price, the flows would cease.

Guido Carli of the Bank of Italy made a presumably face-saving suggestion to the U.S. for a *two-price* system. Under the two-tier system, there would be an official price for official gold transactions and a market price for everyone else. Instead of accepting the realities of the market place, Treasury Secretary Henry Fowler couldn't resist waxing enthusiastic about the two-tier system and what it would do for the United States. An obviously skeptical *Barrons* reported:

> The "two-tier" system, so the master financial craftsman recently boasted about his dubious handi-work, will endure for decades. Frederic L. Deming, Under Secretary of the Treasury, outdid his boss by predicting that it would last "till hell freezes over."*

Within three years of the Fowler-Deming boasts, the two-tier system for gold pricing ended with suspension of convertibility and devaluation of the dollar. In a straight contest between an "official price" and a "market price," once again, as on innumerable occasions in the past five thousand years, the market place won out.

*Barrons, May 27, 1968.

CHAPTER SEVEN
Who Bought All the Gold?

> *[Gold legalization will cause]* a major catastrophe, *of the same magnitude as a Martian invasion or a nuclear attack. . . .*

Treasury Deputy Undersecretary Jack F. Bennett, commenting on proposed legalization of gold ownership for Americans.

THE LETHAL VIEWS ON GOLD held by the Washington-New York Establishment, as exemplified in the above statement, are an interesting contrast with the brave assertion that gold is being phased out of the monetary system. These frightened cries sound more like the truth — a grudging admission that the paper dollar is in danger of being demonetized by gold. The United States owns the world's largest stock of gold and, all Treasury threats to the contrary, has given no real indication it intends to auction it all off tomorrow morning. All Treasury gold auctions held so far have been half-hearted, amateurish, possibly even illegal* sales designed to depress the price rather than to dispose of gold or to raise funds.

---

*See Appendix A.

The U.S. Gold Reserves

The United States has a stock of gold of over 250 million ounces. According to the Bureau of the Mint "Inventory of Gold Bars," the unaudited gold stocks on November 30, 1973 consisted of the following:

TABLE 7-1: U.S. GOLD STOCK (1973)

Fineness 995-999

Size of Bar	Total Bars	Total Ounces
5 oz.	530	2,650
10 ''	4,885	48,850
15 ''	18	270
20 ''	13	260
25 ''	5,694	142,350
30 ''	38	1,140
50 ''	7,965	398,250
250 ''	2,131	532,750
400 ''	118,377	47,350,800
	139,651	48,477,320

Fineness 917-994

Size of Bar	Total Bars	Ounces
5 oz.	2	10
10 ''	2	20
15 ''	4	60
20 ''	6	120
25 ''	3	75
30 ''	9	270
50 ''	43	2,150
250 ''	77	19,250
400 ''	2,143	857,200
	2,289	879,155

Fineness 890-916

Size of Bar	Total Bars	Ounces
25 oz.	1	25
50 "	3	150
250 "	318	79,500
400 "	515,060	206,024,000
	515,382	206,103,675

The most significant conclusion from the above figures is that the bulk of U.S. gold reserves are not in "good delivery" specie. Only 19 percent is more than .995 pure. Most of the stock is in "coin melt" bars of less than .900 fineness. Here is a summary of the above figures:

TABLE 7-2: DISTRIBUTION OF U.S. GOLD, BY FINENESS

Fineness	No. of Bars	Total Weight (ounces)	% of Total (by weight)
995-999	139,651	48,477,320	19.0
917-994	2,289	879,155	0.3
890-916	515,382	206,103,675	80.7
TOTAL	657,322	255,460,150	100.0

There is a most important point to be read into the above Bureau of the Mint statistics. Any Treasury gold sales are likely to be bars of a fineness between .890 and .916. This would mean that the purchaser would need to have the bars refined to .995 to .999, to become "good delivery" bullion. In brief, more than eighty percent of the Treasury stock is not "good delivery" gold, as it is known on the world markets, and thus cannot command the price of good delivery gold. Moreover, because of the necessity to have any purchases refined, the Treasury is likely to encounter less than normal demand for its stock. Good delivery bars (400-ounce bars with a fineness of .995-.999) owned by the United States total 118,377 bars weighing 47 million ounces (less any bars sold since 1973). The bulk of the stock (80 percent) comprises 515,060 bars of 400 ounces with a fineness of .890-.916.

The value of the U.S. stock dropped to $10 billion (at $35 an ounce) in 1971, but has since moved above this figure to $11.8 billion.

European Central Banks Build their Gold Reserves

While the Treasury and IMF economists have been busy claiming that gold is demonitized and on the way out of the international monetary system, the European central banks have been busy quietly following a quite different approach. There was a dramatic shift in European central bank gold holdings in the decade 1960 to 1970. (See Table 7-3 below.) The major outflows of gold in the world were from the Federal Reserve Bank in the United States ($6,734 million) and the Bank of England ($1,452 million), a total of $8,186 million.

This Anglo-American outflow was almost balanced by an inflow of gold *to the central banks* of Continental Europe. France absorbed $1,891 million, West Germany $1,009 million, Italy $684 million, Switzerland $546 million, Austria $421 million, Portugal $350 million, the Netherlands $336 million, Spain $320 million, and Belgium $300 million. This inflow totals $6,142 million, or about three-quarters of the Anglo-American loss. Other major countries also increased their gold holdings; for example, South Africa recorded a net increase of $488 million, Japan $285 million, and Saudi Arabia $101 million during the same period. Even Communist Yugoslavia increased its gold holdings from $4 to $51 million.

In sum, the outflow of gold in the decade of the 1960s came from a very limited geographical area: the Anglo-American Atlantic Alliance. But the inflow of gold was widely distributed: it included virtually all of the major countries of Continental

Europe, as well as important trading countries outside Europe. In terms of numbers of countries, the pro-gold (that is, the gold-absorbing) bloc far outnumbered the anti-gold bloc, as indicated by a willingness to acquire and use gold as a reserve asset.

TABLE 7-3: CHANGES IN CENTRAL BANK GOLD HOLDINGS 1960-1970 AND 1970-1975

Decrease in Total Gold Holdings

(million U.S. dollars at $35 per ounce)

Country	1960	1970	1975	1960/ 1970	1970/ 1975
United States	17,804	11,070	11,401	-6,734	+331
United Kingdom	2,801	1,349	909	-1,452	- 440
Brazil	287	45	57	- 245	+ 7
Canada	885	791	895	- 94	+104
Colombia	78	17	37	- 61	+ 20
Denmark	197	64	74	- 43	+ 10
New Zealand	35	1	1	- 34	0

Increase in Total Gold Holdings

(million U.S. dollars at $35 per ounce)

Country	1960	1970	1975	1960/ 1970	1970/ 1975
France	1,641	3,532	4,113	+1,891	+581
FDR	2,971	3,980	4,792	+1,009	+812
Italy	2,203	2,887	3,361	+ 684	+474
Switzerland	2,185	2,731	3,390	+ 546	+659
South Africa	178	666	741	+ 488	+75
Austria	293	714	851	+ 421	+137
Portugal	552	902	1,135	+ 350	+233
Netherlands	1,451	1,787	2,213	+ 336	+426
Spain	178	498	581	+ 320	+83
Belgium	1,170	1,470	1,718	+ 300	+248
Japan	247	532	860	+ 285	+328
Lebanon	119	288	376	+ 169	+285
Saudi Arabia	18	119	126	+ 101	+ 7
Australia	147	239	306	+ 92	+155
Yugoslavia	4	51	60	+ 47	+ 9

Source: U.S. Department of Commerce Publication, *Statistical Abstract of the United States, 1972,* (Washington, D.C.: Bureau of the

Census, 1972), p. 833, and International Monetary Fund, *International Financial Statistics, December 1975*, (Washington, D.C.: December 1975), Volume XXVIII, Number 12.

See also: J. Aron, *Gold Statistics and Analysis, October 1975*, (New York: J. Aron & Company, Inc., 1975), Table V-F, for similar statistics in troy ounces. Other countries not listed above include: Iraq (+46), Philippines (+41), Taiwan (+41), Greece (+40), and Mexico (+40).

In the next five-year period, 1970 to 1975, the U.S. program to demonetize gold was promoted vigorously at the International Monetary Fund by the United States, but much less enthusiastically by other countries. The 1975 statistics on central-bank gold holdings suggest that the United States and Great Britain are now almost alone in their program to demonetize gold; and even these two countries may be having some second thoughts. Every country that increased its gold holdings in the decade 1960-1970 also increased its gold holdings during the next five years, 1970-1975. Further, the rate of increase in acquisitions is increasing for many important countries, as reflected in the following table:

TABLE 7-4: RELATIVE INCREASE IN GOLD HOLDINGS, 1960-70 VERSUS 1970-75

Percent Increase in Central Bank Gold Holdings

Country	1970 compared to 1960	1975 compared to 1970 (adjusted)
France	+115.2 percent	+32.9 percent
West Germany	+ 34.0 ''	+40.8 ''
Italy	+ 21.5 ''	+32.8 ''
Switzerland	+ 25.0 ''	+48.3 ''
Portugal	+ 63.0 ''	+51.7 ''
Netherlands	+ 23.2 ''	+47.4 ''
Belgium	+ 25.6 ''	+33.7 ''
Japan	+115.4 ''	+123.3 ''
Denmark	- 40.2 ''	+ 31.3 ''

Source: Calculated from data in Table 7-3.

These statistics suggest that the United States is now fighting a lonely — and losing — battle against gold as a reserve asset.

Every major central bank in Europe except pro-gold France is not only increasing its gold reserves, but its *rate* of increase is on the rise. Even Denmark, which reported a 40-percent loss in the decade 1960-1970, turned around and increased its holdings by 31 percent between 1970 and 1975.

Nor are these minor increases of insignificant amounts. West Germany shows a more than + 40-percent increase from 1970 to 1975, compared to + 34-percent rise in the previous decade, Switzerland, a whopping + 48.3 percent jump, compared to + 25 percent in the decade before 1970. Portugal increased her holdings + 63 percent in the 1960-1970 decade and another + 51 percent during the next five years. Netherlands increased her reserves almost + 48 percent in 1970-1975, Belgium almost + 34 percent, France almost + 33 percent, Italy almost + 33 percent. Both Portugal and Italy have since put their gold reserves to good use by raising loans with gold as collateral.

In brief, IMF statistics confirm that far from demonetizing gold by reducing its role as a reserve asset, the central banks of Europe are increasing their holdings of gold as a reserve asset. Moreover, not a single major European central bank is an exception to this observation. Even England, with its dire economic troubles and scary balance-of-payments deficits, managed to increase its gold holdings from a low of $800 million in 1972 to over $900 million in 1975. We have already pointed out that Kuwait refused to supply oil in exchange for British sterling, but is adding to *its* gold reserves. This turn-around by Britain on gold is none too soon, and may be too late.

The position of the Arab countries in general is more puzzling. All Middle East Arab countries — including the Arab socialist countries — increased their gold holdings in the five-year period 1970-1975, although the distribution of this increase is not what pro-gold readers might expect:

TABLE 7-5: CHANGE IN GOLD HOLDINGS OF ARAB COUNTRIES 1970 TO 1975 (IN MILLION U.S. DOLLARS)

Country	1970	1975	Change
Lebanon	191	223	+ 88 million $
Kuwait	86	148	+ 62 ″ ″
Algeria	191	223	+ 32 ″ ″

Iraq	144	167	+23	''	''
Iran	131	153	+22	''	''
Libya	85	99	+14	''	''
Egypt	93	105	+12	''	''
Saudi Arabia	119	128	+9	''	''
Jordan	28	33	+5	''	''
Syria	28	33	+5	''	''

Source: International Monetary Fund, *International Financial Statistics*, December 1975, (Washington, D.C.: December 1975).

Given the inflation in the oil-buying countries of the West, it had been predicted that the Arabs would demand payment in a form likely to retain the value of their oil receipts over the long run. Gold had been suggested as the logical asset; but gold requires storage and does not provide a return on capital, while the Arabs traditionally have a preference for a yield on investments. Consequently, the major oil-producing countries of Saudi Arabia and Iran increased their gold holdings only nominally: $9 million for Saudi Arabia and $22 million for Iran. These are trifling increases, when compared to their torrent of foreign currencies from oil sales. United States influence in these counties is a conceivable explanation. On the other hand, little oil producer Kuwait increased its gold holdings $62 million in five years. Lebanon, a center of gold trading and coin counterfeiting, increased its gold holdings by $88 million in five years. In sum, the Arab central banks — by contrast to wealthy Arab individuals — are not gold hoarders.

And the United States? In the face of all the political bravado from the Treasury about demonetizing gold and selling off the Fort Knox gold stocks as barbaric relics not worth the storage space, the United States increased its gold holdings from just above the psychological bench mark of $10 billion in 1972 to around $12 billion in early 1975. (Holdings went down again slightly towards the end of 1975.) *The United States is not, despite the Washington bombast, selling off its gold — at least, not yet.* On the contrary, the United States is apparently trying to preserve its gold stocks while keeping the price down with a barrage of anti-gold propaganda!

Why hasn't the U.S. Treasury kept to its public word and

sold off the Fort Knox gold stock? Simply because every Washington economist, and maybe even a few of the politicians, know about Gresham's Law, and the stark reality of Gresham's Law could drive every Washington economist (and politician) from his plush job to rifling in garbage cans for survival.

"Bad Money Always Drives Out Good"

What is Gresham's Law?

For many centuries governments have passed laws to create legal tender; most of these laws have been accompanied by vicious penalties for the use of gold and silver in lieu of state-decreed money, whether such "legal tender" be paper or a debased coinage. However, never yet has any government that decreed what people will use as money succeeded in having that decree accepted in the market place. The usual circumstance that leads to non-acceptance of a government-decreed money is a coinage that has been debased or is intrinsically worth less than its face value in gold and silver. When such "bad money" has circulated side by side with "good" or acceptable money, history demonstrates that bad money *always* drives out good.

This observation is normally attributed to Sir Thomas Gresham (1518-1579), but the empirical fact had been noted centuries earlier. In 405 B.C. the Greek Aristophanes commented on the behavior of the emergency money then circulated in Athens: "In our Republic," said Aristophanes, "bad citizens are preferred to good, just as bad money circulates while good money disappears."*

In the fourteenth century, Bishop Oresme of Lisieux in France noted the outflow of French coins after the coinage had been debased. The Polish scientist Copernicus made similar observations. It was the nineteenth century English economist Macleod who quoted a letter written by Sir Thomas Gresham to Queen Elizabeth, describing the phenomenon; and so history has named this consequence Gresham's Law:

"It may please Your Majesty to understand," he writes, *"that the first occasion of the fall of the Ex-*

Frogs 717, sqq. Cited in A. R. Burns, *op. cit.*, p. 467.

*change did grow by the King's Majesty, your late
Father, in abasing his coin from vi ounces fine to iii
ounces fine. Whereupon the Exchange fell from xxvis
viiid to xiiis ivd, which was the occasion that all your
fine gold was conveyed out of this your realm."**

This is a crude expression of what is more generally known
today as Gresham's Law. Gresham's Law states simply that "bad
money drives out good money," and there are almost innumerable examples to support its validity. In other words, if gold and
paper money circulate together, then gold will be kept out of
circulation and hoarded while paper fiat money will be passed on
as quickly as possible. Ludwig von Mises phrased it another way:

*It would be more correct to say that the money
which the government's decree has undervalued disappears from the market and the money which the decree has overvalued remains.†*

All of which means that, while there may be millions of $20
paper Federal Reserve notes in circulation today, just try to find a
single $20 gold coin!

This suggests why a paper-factory, legal money system must
be enforced by the police power of the state to survive. Certainly, a paper system will not last in open competition with gold
and silver coins. It is recognition of Gresham's Law that forces the
U.S. Treasury to be vehemently against the issue of *any* gold
coins, even an innocuous gold bicentennial memorial coin. While
at the same time the Treasury *must* keep a damper on the price of
gold in the market place.

The Treasury must destroy the credibility of gold at all costs.
This is a war with no quarter. Only one money medium can survive. The victor will be either a paper dollar or a gold dollar.

William Cobbett, in his classic *Paper Against Gold*, described
the inevitability of the war on gold this way:

*While the money of any country consists of
nothing but these scarce metals; while it consists of*

---

*Human Action, p. 447.

†Cited in F. R. Salter, *Sir Thomas Gresham, (1518-1579)*, (London: Leonard Parsons,
n.d.), p. 37.

*nothing but gold and silver, there is no fear of its be-
coming too abundant; but, if the money of a country be
made of lead, tin, wood, leather or paper; and if anyone
can make it, who may choose to make it, there needs no
extraordinary vision to foresee, that there will be a great
abundance of this sort of money, and that the gold and
silver money, being in fact, no longer of any use in such
a state of things, will go, either into the hoards of the
prudent, or into the bags of those who have the means of
sending or carrying them to those foreign countries
where they are wanted, and where they will bring their
value.**

The principle applies not only to competition between gold
and paper, as noted by William Cobbett, but also to lesser differences, for example even between gold coins of differing fineness.
In the United States between 1814 and 1834, gold coins, although
minted, were rarely seen in circulation. Increasing gold prices
made the bullion content worth more than the face value of the
coin. (For example, a $1 gold dollar could exchange for $1.02 in
silver.) Consequently, gold eagles and half-eagles went into the
melting pot or underneath the mattress. One interesting result is
the numismatic rarity of these coins today. Joel D. Rettew estimates that although 1.2 million gold half-eagles were issued between 1814 and 1834, only 500 to 700 have survived in the U.S.
down to the present day. The remainder were exported or melted
for their bullion value. The only survivors were coins put aside as
collectors' pieces or family heirlooms.†

In other words, Gresham's Law operates inexorably in all
countries, under all conditions, at all times. This is why the U.S.
cannot dispose of its gold stock and cannot even allow gold to circulate in fair competition with the monopoly of Federal Reserve
paper money.

Recognition of Gresham's Law is one thing. The vicious
retribution wreaked by the U.S. monetary authorities on gold preferrers is quite another. Let's now turn to a case of official ven-

---

*William Cobbett, *op. cit.*, p. 4.

†"Gresham's Law explains shortage of U.S. half eagles of 1814-1834," by Joel D.
Rettew. *Coin World*, January 14, 1976.

geance against one such group of gold preferrers: the American
Institute Counselors, led by Colonel Edward C. Harwood of Great
Barrington, Massachusetts.

American Institute Counselors and the SEC

For many years Colonel E. C. Harwood, a retired U.S. Army
officer, and the American Institute for Economic Research at
Great Barrington, Massachusetts have presented the "hard
money" case. The A.I.E.R. was quite outspoken in its warnings of
the dangers of imposing socialism on the back of a fiat-money
system.*

Founded before World War II, the A.I.E.R. and its com-
panion organization, the American Institute Counselors,
represented some of the sophisticated few who had read enough
history to reason independently of the Establishment propaganda barrage and, even more rare, to act on the basis of their
own conclusions. Unfortunately, the A.I.C. investors ran afoul of
some Establishment laws designed to "protect" such mavericks
from their own conclusions.

Any person who followed the broad A.I.E.R. advice would
not only have protected his wealth; he would also have enjoyed
substantial capital gains. Colonel Harwood was recommending
investments in gold when it was $35.00 an ounce; and he was
doing so with a flood of statistical evidence and reasoning that
puts much of our modern writing in the field of monetary theory
to shame.

This is probably where Col. Harwood made his mistake. Not
only did his clients make money over the long run, but there was
a logical reinforcement for his arguments. By contrast, the stock
market, the mutual funds, and Establishment investment advisers have been about as useful over the long run as sticking pins
into the lists of stocks that appear in your daily newspaper.

Back in 1958 the American Investment Counselors recommended gold for ten percent of a portfolio. During the recent bear
stock market, the A.I.C. recommended selling *all* common stocks,
and placing 30 percent of these assets in Swiss annuities, and the

---

*See bibliography for list of some A.I.E.R. publications.

balance in gold-related reserves. Thus, A.I.C. customers avoided the pitfalls of the bear stock market, profited from the rise in gold from $35 an ounce to the $130-range, and also benefited from the upvaluation of the Swiss franc.*

The other side of this mouth-watering coin is that Colonel Harwood admits that he has nothing but contempt for government regulation of securities, and scorns normal accounting procedures, "audits and glossy annual reports and all that stuff." Here was a heretic who was flouting all the government-ordained conventions. The crux of the question was whether the 3,500 or so investors guided by A.I.C. had the right to invest with whomever they wished, with or without the doubtful benefits of the regulations promulgated by the Securities and Exchange Commission. The SEC said No!

So far as the war on gold is concerned, there were no complaints about Colonel Harwood *before* the SEC moved into action. The affair of the SEC and American Institute Counselors is an integral part of the propaganda campaign against gold and gold-oriented proponents conducted by the U.S. Government.† As the *Wall Street Journal* reported on December 10, 1975:

> *One question is to what extent, if any, the claims of American gold investors exceed the assets held by the bank. The SEC, however, has received hundreds of letters supporting Mr. Harwood and it hasn't heard from anyone so far who believes that he has been cheated, SEC lawyers acknowledge.*

Compare Colonel Harwood's record to the SEC record. Of 8000 new corporate stocks registered by the SEC in the five years 1969-1974 and sold over the counter, nearly one-half declined an average of 87 percent from their peaks; in mid-1974 *current quotations could be found for less than ten percent* of their one-time approved registrations.

---

*Detailed recommendations and history can be found in "Who is guarding the interests of investors?" American Institute Counselors, Inc., October 11, 1974.

† The reader would appreciate "Malefactor or Martyr- In the Harwood affair, more questions than answers," *Barrons*, February 23, 1976.

Contrasting the record of gold-oriented A.I.C. with the government's watchdog agency, the Securities and Exchange Commission, reveals that the SEC has presided over the *loss* to the general public of an astronomical fortune (a decline of $42 billion in over-the-counter stocks alone); while the A.I.C. has quietly protected the financial interests of its relatively few followers.

With a timing that can hardly be coincidental, the SEC decided to eliminate Colonel Harwood and his too-successful competition. In November 1975 the SEC charged Harwood, A.I.C., A.I.E.R., and related organizations (including the Swiss Credit Bank) with "flagrant and near total disregard" of American securities laws. Violations, said the SEC, "covered virtually the entire panoply of federal securities laws, including the registration, anti-fraud and record-keeping provisions." In all, the hostile SEC report against Harwood ran to 94 pages.*

Several months later, Judge Gesell of the U.S. District Court, Washington, D.C. ordered ". . . that this action as it affects Harwood is hereby terminated with prejudice . . .", meaning that the SEC must not again make such charges. Colonel Harwood remained in the case in order to fulfill what he sees as his moral obligation to the investors.

The reaction of European central bankers to Washington's war on gold could not be controlled by the U.S. Government. A small American group of sophisticated investors could be stopped, however . . . and was.

Having looked at developments in both arenas, it is now time to survey the huge mountain of illiquid debt which has been generated by the imposition of a more "flexible" money supply in the U.S. and the abandonment of the gold standard.

---

*The author attempted to obtain the SEC complaint and copies of any written complaints submitted by A.I.C. investors *before* the SEC moved against Harwood. On the first attempt (citing the Freedom of Information Act), the author was sent only the countercomplaint by Harwood; the matter of investors' complaints was not even answered. A second application, with a copy to Congresswoman Bella Abzug, yielded the author a copy of *one* letter, written on February 22, 1976 (that is, *after* the SEC moved into court). This letter complained about the SEC action, not Colonel Harwood!

CHAPTER EIGHT

Cracks in the Debt Structure

> *While we have difficulties here and there, the American people can rest assured that our banking system is sound.*

Arthur Burns, Chairman, Federal Reserve System, on ABC-TV, January 18, 1976.

OBVIOUSLY, SOMETHING OF MONUMENTAL PROPORTIONS is scaring the operators of the Federal Reserve paper factory. A one-time Federal Reserve manager has presented the best explanation of the inevitable (and scary) forthcoming crisis.

Exter's Debt Pyramid

John Exter, one-time manager of gold operations for the Federal Reserve Bank of New York, and currently a vocal advocate for a return to gold, has an easily understandable presentation of our illiquid debt-money structure and its latent danger.* Exter compares the domestic debt structure to an inverted pyramid.

The pyramid represents all debt and money in the U.S., when visualized as a closed economic system. The pyramid grows

---

*It is not, however, original with Exter. An early crude version appeared in Irving Fisher, *100% Money*, (New York: Adelphi, 1936), p. 50.

CHART 8-1: THE DEBT PYRAMID

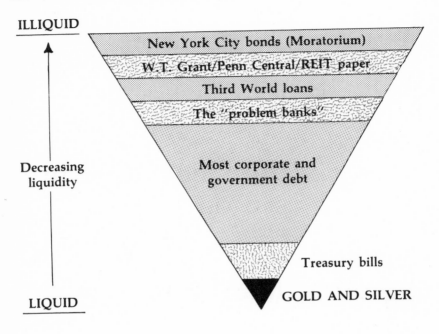

ILLIQUID

New York City bonds (Moratorium)

W.T. Grant/Penn Central/REIT paper

Third World loans

The "problem banks"

Most corporate and government debt

Decreasing liquidity

Treasury bills

LIQUID   **GOLD AND SILVER**

with government deficit spending not funded from taxation, continuing Federal Reserve debt creation, and all debts incurred by corporations and individuals. Layers of the inverted pyramid represent varying degrees of liquidity, defined as the ability to realize assets to pay off unexpected calls for payment of debt. Gold is the most liquid of assets, and one for which a market is always available at some price. So the tip or bottom of the pyramid represents the relatively minute amount of monetized gold in our monetary system held as reserves (presently $12 billion at $35 an ounce) compared to the overwhelming amount of fiat money instruments and credit.

Moving upward toward the base or top of the pyramid are more and more illiquid layers of paper debt which are increasingly *less* convertible into liquid assets. For example, the debt of such corporations as Lockheed and Penn Central, where the Federal Government has come to the rescue, or of New York City municipals, where a moratorium has made the debt non-convertible, is located at the broad inverted base of the pyramid. Thus far, problems at this illiquid base have been "solved" (that is, postponed) by government intervention, not by allowing liquidation of the offending institutions, which would strengthen the financial structure as a whole.

The extraordinary nature of the entire debt-structure problem can be capsulized by noting that as far back as *1919* Federal Reserve Board member Adolphe C. Miller wrote to Benjamin Strong, Governor of Federal Reserve Bank of New York, about the inflation *to that point* and concluded, ". . . There has got to be liquidation."*

The survival of this multi-trillion dollar debt pyramid depends on maintaining public confidence, a topic we have already discussed. Any breach of confidence will bring about attempted liquidation of paper debts, certainly these debts near the upper broad region of the pyramid, and conversion into more liquid assets — Treasury bills or even gold. This conversion becomes increasingly difficult, because the ratio of gold to assets represented by paper is constantly declining, due to the unrelenting expansion of debt by the Federal Reserve System. Moreover, unless the Fed pumps in more funds (*i.e.*, maintains liquidity by continuing expansion of the monetary base), the pyramid will collapse.

According to Exter's reasoning, because of the size and complexity of the American economy, and because the U.S. has the largest number of illiquid debtors (and, Exter might have added, the largest number of "free lunch" promoters), the coming squeeze will be the most intense in U.S. history. A series of cracks in confidence will appear and start spreading as firms and individuals find themselves unable to repay debts. At some point, probably at a time of soaring interest rates, a crisis in liquidity will follow a particularly spectacular failure which the Fed has been unable to prevent by pouring in paper dollars. (New York City is an obvious candidate to be such a catalyst.) Creditors will then attempt to become more liquid; and no matter how many reserves the Fed provides, the banks will fear to make loans. This situation is known colloquially as "pushing on a string." At some

---

*Percy L. Greaves, Jr., *Understanding the Dollar Crisis*, (Boston: Western Islands Publishers, 1973), p. 198.

point panic sets in and the structure plunges into a deflationary spiral.

This is not a pretty picture. And it is made uglier by a stream of mouthy politicians thumping and roaring for more give-away programs to get themselves re-elected. But why should Hubert Humphrey and Jacob Javits worry? *Aprés Hubert et Jacob, le deluge!*

Let's take a brief look at the more important of the illiquid layers in the debt pyramid and their recent behaviour; it is failures in the debt structure that gives us a fairly good estimate of how far along the road to final collapse we now find ourselves.

Corporate Failures

A few well-publicized corporate failures during the 1974-1975 depression, such as the W. T. Grant department store chain and Penn Central Railroad, overshadow the general observation that corporate failures have not yet been substantial; they have in fact been only slightly above the normal averages. It is usual for the bankruptcy rate to increase during depressions. This is the market's way of flushing out inefficient operations and reshuffling inappropriately applied capital.

Not surprisingly, the first signs of large-scale corporate failures in the mid-1970s showed up in the regulated sector, where decades of government regulation had forced inefficient application of capital resources or held down the return on capital, with the consequence of under-investment and protection of inefficient practices.

Except for the W. T. Grant chain store retailer, with over $600 million of bank loans, collapses in the 1974-75 depression were concentrated in transportation, particularly the long-ailing, over-regulated railroads (Penn Central) and near collapse in the equally over-regulated major airlines (Pan American and TWA).

Why did the Pennsylvania Central Railroad System file for bankruptcy? Mainly because the Interstate Commerce Commission wouldn't allow Penn Central to drop unremunerative lines and the ICC rate regulation guaranteed inadequate returns, insufficient to maintain equipment and trackage. In brief, the natural advantages of railroads for freight traffic were strangled by ICC regulation. The Penn Central finally owed $130 million in property taxes and $20 million in corporate taxes. What would happen to a small businessman who defaulted on a tax debt of just $100? You can be sure there would be threatening letters, visits by abusive Federal revenue officers, perhaps even seizure of property — and all without the benefit of the courts and the usual constitutional protections. But what happened to an illiquid Penn Central? Government subsidies!

Another potential debt disaster-area comprises the airlines system, which is "protected" by government regulation and overextended in capacity. The three major airlines in difficulties in 1975 were Eastern, Pan American, and TWA. Of course, Pan American instituted an effective program of cutbacks and cost-cutting, and by the end of 1975 Pan Am showed a profit. TWA, with over a $1 billion long-term debt and a loss-making operation, was in worse shape. Eastern, with almost $800 million in long-term debt, averted default only by deferring about $75 million of repayments until 1977. At the other end of the airlines debt-spectrum were United and Northwestern, both with a healthy cash position. The major airlines had $5.8 billion of long-term debt outstanding at the end of 1975; they take up a fair-sized slice of the Exter debt pyramid and are prime candidates for trouble in the *next* liquidity squeeze.

Real Estate Failures

The collapsing debt structure in England during the past few years has featured a major collapse in property values. This suggests the possibility of similar collapse in the United States. Indeed, a part of the real estate market (the REITs, or Real Estate Investment Trusts) did collapse recently, emphasizing the peculiar vulnerability of real estate for the banking structure, particularly in New York City. In 1975 a wave of foreclosures hit Manhattan business properties. In September 1975 Massachusetts Mutual filed to foreclose on the Chrysler Building. The Royal Manhattan Hotel was auctioned off in November. Several office towers are now vacant and the New York Board of Real Estate noted a major drop in the prices of apartment buildings that were sold, down substantially from the 180-percent of assessed value in 1975. The root cause was a predatory city government, rent control, and burdensome taxes imposed by New York politicians.

The REIT collapse in the 1974-1975 depression demonstrates the almost pathetically weak loan policies of our major banks. The fate of these real estate investment trusts sponsored by banks can be measured by the collapse in their stock market prices:

TABLE 8-1: STOCK MARKET PRICES OF REITs, 1972-1975

REIT	Affiliated Parent Bank	Price at End 1972	Price at End 1975
Chase Manhattan and Realty	Chase Manhattan Bank	$70.00	$3.00
Continental Illinois Realty	Continental Illinois National Bank	$25.00	$1.50
Wells Fargo Mortgage Investors	Wells Fargo	$30.00	$5.00

Chase Manhattan Mortgage and Realty, the largest real estate investment trust, which is sponsored by the Chase Manhattan Bank, employed Chase Bank as a consultant under an advisory contract. Listed on the New York Exchange, the Chase Manhattan REIT peaked at $70.00 in 1972, and was just holding its neck above water in late 1975 at $3.00 per share.

The careless, unrealistic investment approach of the major banks typified by Chase is of critical importance as the banks themselves could trigger a deflationary collapse. For example, Chase is a popular holding for bank certificates of deposit held by "liquid assets" funds: In November 1975 Dreyfus Liquid Assets, Inc. held $13 million of Chase negotiable paper; the smaller Scudder Managed Reserves, Inc. held $4 million of Chase's paper; and other liquid funds held quantities of Chase paper in about the same proportions to their sizes.

As a temporary measure to keep the REITs afloat, the banks resorted to mortgage and real estate swaps with affiliated REIT subsidiaries. The banks took over REIT property, often at an inflated, unrealistically high valuation, and canceled the mortgage debt. The banks look for future inflation to bail them out of the problem before it becomes obvious that absorption of shaky real-estate assets only compounds the banks' own structural problems. It is fascinating to note the superficial way in which the REIT problem has been swept under the carpet. As a Securities and Exchange Commission accountant remarked, "When a creditor swaps a loan for property, it's not an arm's length transaction. There's a real question of Mickey Mouse accounting."*

The bankers undertaking the "Mickey Mouse accounting" are the same bankers who operate the Federal Reserve System and control the U.S. economy on a day-to-day basis!

In all, about 44 REITs are in liquidity trouble; they owe the banks about $8 billion, and the creditor banks are counting on inflation to bail them out of their 20 to 25-percent overpriced real estate assets. The REIT problem constitutes a significant layer of Exter's debt pyramid; it is in serious trouble and has yet to impact fully the financial structure.

Municipal Failures

The prime contemporary example of collapse in the municipal debt structure is the decline and fall of New York City, which is dragging New York State along behind.

There is nothing new about monetary chaos in New York City. A century ago, a State Assemblyman complained in 1877 that, "in the past it has been impossible to get at the figures with any degree of accuracy."† Back in 1908 Edgar J. Levey published his *New York City's Progress Towards Bankruptcy* in which he detailed New York City's inability to stay within budgets. Levy cited a rate of expenditure three times that of its population growth, with much of the expenditures siphoned off by a corrupt government. Almost 70 years ago, Levey predicted ultimate collapse of the city's tax base and bankruptcy.

By the early 1970s New York City had run out of political gimmicks and pressure plays. In October 1975 decades of inefficiency, profligate spending, periodically crying wolf to attract

---

Wall Street Journal, January 5, 1976.

†*New York Herald*, January 23, 1877.

Federal and taxpayer assistance, all came to a boiling climax. In good old-fashioned New York-style, the politicos headlined the city's financial crisis — only this time no one came running to help. New York City finally faced bankruptcy, and much of the United States couldn't care less. The gut issue, which was not publicly discussed but which affected all talk of "solutions," was that New York City forms an important layer in Exter's pyramid; the failure of New York City could bring the entire U.S. debt-structure tumbling down in short order.

From the end of October to the end of December 1975, the city had a cash shortage of $1 billion (even without servicing its debts) and it had no way to raise anything like that amount. About two-thirds of the city's $12.3 billion long-term debt, and one-half of its short-term debt, was held by individuals. Commercial banks held almost $3 billion of New York City paper. In November the State Legislature passed a moratoriam on $1.6 billion of New York City notes, suspending payments for three years. This hit hard at the small investors in New York, not the banks, because it was these "little people" who had enough faith in their political leaders to invest $10,000 in a note and believe the inscription printed on its face: "The City of New York — . . . promises to pay the bearer the sum of $10,000 on the due date specified above in lawful money of the United States of America."

For a multitude of these investors, realization of the worthlessness of their paper assets came too late. And while Congress will bail out a Penn Central, it is not about to rush to the aid of a single person, or even several people, who have no political clout but just happen to own a $10,000 New York City note.

Following predictable face-saving protests by President Ford that the Federal Government would never, never bail out New York City, Washington came to the rescue in November 1975 with $2.3 billion per year in direct Federal loans. They were coupled to a minimal program for the city to cut back spending and get its finances in order. Federal aid is doled out month by month, with all outstanding loans supposedly to be repaid at the end of each fiscal year until the program ends in June 1978.

Just four weeks prior to this action, President Ford had said he would veto any bailout plan and he actually urged bankruptcy legislation for the city. What changed the President's mind? Obviously, someone told him the grim truth about the debt pyramid, and the probable rippling effect of a financial collapse by New York City.

New York State, which ran $1.6 billion in the red for fiscal 1975, also came to the aid of New York City and promptly got bogged down in the same monetary mire. The State has over $4 billion outstanding of "full faith and credit" debt, plus another $10 billion of long-term, "moral obligation" bonds, issued largely under Governor Nelson Rockefeller (in probable contravention of the State Constitution). In December 1975 the State tried to float a minor issue of $9.5 million of transportation bonds — and received no bids.

So the New York story is by no means over. The choice is clear: either the Federal Government continues to bail out the city, magnifying its own problems if it does so, or another portion of the debt pyramid faces collapse.

Foreign Loan Failures

Added to the problems of corporate failures, collapse of the real estate market in New York (as well as in the United Kingdom, where U.S. banks have sizeable investments), and a moratorium on New York City bonds, American banks also have substantial loans outstanding in Third World underdeveloped countries.

In 1973 the 86 developing countries had a combined overseas debt of about $145 billion. Of this, about $17.8 billion was owed to banks, mostly the big New York banks. This included $5 billion (some say $12 billion) to Chase Manhattan, possibly the same (some reports say more) at Citibank, and about $2 billion at Manufacturers Hanover Trust Bank. Most of the underdeveloped countries are running heavy balance-of-payment deficits and are not major oil producers. Third World countries need $8 billion, over and above their combined $35 billion deficits, just to service the interest on their private bank loans; this does not include any repayment of the principle.

One major debtor is Argentina, which owes about $8 billion abroad. Given its internal political and economic problems, there is a heavy probability of failure for at least a substantial portion of the debt. A number of countries in Africa are in debt; Zaire, for example, has an external debt of about $1 billion and is in default. In Asia, Korea has an external debt of just under $6 billion and seems destined for default. The Indonesian government oil agency, Pertamina, has run up a monumental debt of $10.5 billion.

Much of the debt not held by New York banks is held by Robert McNamara's World Bank. The portfolios of the International Bank for Reconstruction and Development include loans to 23 of the poorest countries, as listed by the United Nations, and McNamara is promoting schemes for vast increases in loans to all of them. Of course, all such loans to a significant extent are guaranteed by the U.S. Government, which create *another* hidden time bomb ticking away beneath the Federal Reserve System. For instance, one contemporary World Bank project is to move 1.5 million people from Java to another Indonesian island, Sumatra, at a cost of $750 million; one quarter of this amount is guaranteed by the U.S. taxpayer.*

Domestic Bank Failures

All these major illiquid sectors place burdens on the U.S. banking structure and so set the stage for an overall collapse. The failure of an *individual* bank is a signal that the system is automatically ridding itself of weak, inefficient, or badly run units. Failure is a normal phenomenon, although hardly welcome to depositors and shareholders. Banks always fail in a depression or in times of tight money; but bank failures were by no means as common in the gold-standard era of the nineteenth century as they have been in the paper-money era of this century. Under the discipline of gold, the incentive to wildly over-expand the banking system does not exist, and consequently there are fewer weak units to be flushed out.

The financial panics of 1877, 1893, and 1907 brought an increase in bank failures but, except for the 1893 panic, these failures totalled less than 200 banks per year. With the advent of fiat credit systems, not subject to the discipline of the gold standard, bank failures rose substantially: 400 in 1921, more than 2,000 in 1931, and fewer failures — but with considerably larger debts — in

---

Forbes, September 1, 1975, "Too ambitious?"

1974-1976. The institution of the Federal Deposit Insurance Corporation (FDIC) may have eased the fears of small depositors, but there is no guarantee that the FDIC can withstand a 1931-type panic. The FDIC has never been tested with a major banking crisis.

Today, larger banks are failing, albeit in fewer numbers, while the total of bad loans is far greater than it was in the 1930s. The banking problem, the so-called "problem banks," became obvious with the onset of the 1974-1975 depression, which was itself brought on by the inflationary excesses of the 1971-1974 period. One of the first major collapses, in late 1973, was the Beverly Hills National Bank. This bank sold commercial paper issued by its parent, Beverly Hills Bancorp, and when the latter institution was unable to pay interest as it came due, a run on the Beverly Hills National Bank was triggered. Bank assets were promptly sold off to Wells Fargo, a large California bank, which became a "problem bank" itself within two years. Risky commercial paper was also a factor in the 1973 collapse of United States National Bank in San Diego.

With the onset of the 1974-1975 depression, bank failures increased to 15 banks in 1974; they included the collapse of the Franklin National Bank of New York, with total assets of $3.6 billion — the largest bank failure in American history. Deposit liabilities of the Franklin were absorbed by the European-American Bank and Trust Company in October 1974. On the heels of Franklin came failure of the substantial Security National Bank of Long Island (total assets, $1.7 billion). Whereas the prime cause of failure for Franklin National was foreign-exchange transaction losses, the collapse of the real estate loan market and the shaky REIT structure led to the failure of Security National, which was merged with Chemical Bank of New York. Remaining 1974 bank failures were relatively small, ranging from the American City National Bank and Trust Company of Milwaukee, with $188 million in assets, to the Bank of Chidester in Arkansas, with $2.2 million in assets.* These bank failures stem from illiquidity and represent a failure of the debt structure in the upper portion of Exter's inverted pyramid.

---

*For details, see "Bank failures and public policy," by R. Alton Gilbert, in *Review* of the Federal Reserve Bank of St. Louis, November 1975.

The creaking of the banking segment of the debt structure in the Exter pyramid is reflected in the overall bank-failure statistics for the past few years. Deposits of failing banks, as a percentage of total deposits, increased substantially in the late 1960s and early 1970s:*

TABLE 8-2: PERCENT OF TOTAL BANK DEPOSITS LOST, 1967-1974:

Year	Deposits of Commercial Banks[1] (billion $)	Deposits of Failing Banks[2] (thousand $)	(2) as % of (1)
1967	315.6	10,878	0.0034
1968	344.8	22,524	0.0065
1969	360.4	40,133	0.0111
1970	376.2	52,826	0.0140
1971	433.7	132,032	0.0304
1972	484.3	99,786	0.0206
1973	549.6	971,312	0.1767
1974	611.1	1,571,208	0.2571

By 1974, deposits of failing banks represented one quarter of one percent of all bank deposits. Worse news was to surface as the U.S. pulled out of the deepest depression since 1931.

Bank Problems at the Top

In early 1976 the *Washington Post* ran a front-page story with profound implications: Chase Manhattan Bank (the second-largest U.S. bank) and National City Bank (Citibank, the third-largest U.S. bank) — two of the most prestigious and respected Wall Street institutions — were on a Federal list of 150 "problem banks" with a high probability of failure. These "problem banks" require constant overseeing by the Comptroller of the Currency; they are defined as banks whose substandard or "shaky" loans exceed 65 percent of their gross capital funds, including shareholders' equity and loan-loss reserves. In defense of these top-echelon banks, Comptroller Smith argued that the published list

---

Ibid.

was dated mid-1974, and that the banks *remained* on the list only because their problem loans exceeded 65 percent. In other words, their substandard loans were at one time *above* this benchmark figure, and the problems were compounded by other misdeeds.

The most dangerous effect of the *Washington Post* story was the potential for a run on either bank — a run that would ripple outwards to other banks, mutual funds, pension funds, and a myriad of other financial institutions. A "run" on either Chase or Citibank could set the stage for the collapse of the entire U.S. debt structure. If this happened, almost overnight the debt pyramid would crumble, leaving only the tip of gold and other liquid assets intact.

Such a run did not develop. But finally the emerging bank problem was recognized by the regulators. In early 1974 the Federal Reserve took American banks in general to task for mismanagement, under-capitalization, and shaky liability management techniques. In the preceding years, under the assumption that the Fed dare not let the banking system — or even a sizeable unit in the banking system — go to the wall, banks had embarked on a pattern of increasingly more risky loans. According to a 1974 study made by First Albany Corporation in New York, not only had there been a dramatic deterioration in all the ratios by which bank stability is traditionally measured, but there had been a significant increase in short-term borrowing (*i.e.*, certificates of deposit and federal funds). In brief, bankers were lending long and borrowing short, which was about as good a policy to guarantee a collapse as anything they might have done. Between 1964 and 1973, the ratio of capital to deposits for the top ten banks declined from 9.2 percent to 5.5 percent; profit margins fell from twenty percent to eight percent.

In spite of the deterioration in the ratios and margins and all sorts of prior warnings, it was the *Washington Post* that was criticized for publicizing the problem.* One would anticipate that both Chase Manhattan and Citibank would assure that errors were being righted, that in-house procedures had been changed, that conservative caution would be the order of the day from now on. On the contrary, both David Rockefeller, Chairman of the

---

*Wall Street Journal, January 12, 1976.

Board at Chase, and Henry B. Wriston, chairman of Citibank, lashed out at the press for revealing such bank problems. Rockefeller averred: "There is absolutely no question that the bank is sound and profitable — any inference to the contrary is totally irresponsible."* Henry B. Wriston echoed David Rockefeller's comments, blasting the *Washington Post* article as "misleading, irresponsible and at variance with the facts."

An almost unnoticed statement by First National Bank of Boston, the eighteenth largest bank in the United States, throws more ominous light on the banking structure. When the *New York Times* published a "problem" list, the First National Bank of Boston expressed surprise that its name was included as a bank with more than 65 percent bad loans. First National of Boston contended that *their* ratio of loans-to-capital and liabilities-to-capital was "30% below the median of the 20 largest bank holding companies in the country."† The obvious retort is, then what must be the condition of the loan portfolios of banks with less advantageous ratios? By objecting to its relative place on the "watch list," First National merely drew attention to the shakier condition of the other banks on the list.

In any event, Congressman Benjamin Rosenthal promptly announced that the House Operations Subcommittee would hold hearings on Wall Street's precarious financial position. Not to be outdone, Senator William Proxmire announced that the Senate Banking Committee would hold similar hearings — thus providing more publicity, and, from the viewpoint of Rockefeller and Wriston, presumably even more "irresponsible" reporting.

The Washington regulators now began to express concern about the all-important factor of public confidence. What if confidence in these banks was sufficiently shaken to trigger a run on Chase and Citibank? It was recalled that a major factor in the Franklin National collapse was that depositors withdrew $800 million of deposits in a single week. Undoubtedly, a run on one (or both) of the largest of the nation's 14,000 banks would snow-

---

*At about this time, David's brother Nelson was touting a $100-billion energy "plan" to Congress and the press. The New York State debt problem can also be laid at Rocky's doorstep; he apparently has an insatiable appetite for spending other people's money (not his own) on white elephants.

†*Wall Street Journal*, January 23, 1976.

ball into a mammoth financial crisis. Federal Reserve Board chairman Arthur Burns appealed to the Congress not to look closely at the banks, because close inspection would create "enormous" risks of a banking panic. Presumably believing that what you can't see won't hurt you, Burns said:

> When you cast doubt on the solvency of individual banks, you are taking grave risks not only of causing a run on individual banks but also of causing broad tremors in a very large part of our financial system.*

And this, added Burns, would have a ripple effect overseas. But appeals not to look too closely merely underline the fragile nature of the debt pyramid.

TABLE 8-3: SUMMARY OF CRACKS IN THE DEBT PYRAMID AS OF 1976

Sector	Signs of Deflationary Collapse
Corporate sector	Minimal so far. Congress has bailed out problem firms and so postponed collapse.
Real estate sector	REITs so far only serious problem ($11 billion), still to impact the economic structure. Banks are relying on inflation to bale them out. No property-values collapse at the moment.
Municipal sector	New York City has defaulted by its moratorium. More to come.
Foreign loan sector	Not yet impacted. Tanker loans a serious situation ($17 billion). Some Third World countries will default ($30-40 billion). A real mine-field, could easily get out of control.
Domestic bank sector	So far under control. The "runs" in 1975 were controlled by the Fed. Some evidence of a more cautious loan policy, but no appreciation among banks of the fundamental gold-versus-paper problem.

Wall Street Journal, January 22, 1976.

How Much Battering Can the Debt Structure Take?

Under a gold standard, any bank is required to exchange gold for its paper *on demand*. The expectation of demands for gold restrain banks from profligate behavior. Today we have no such discipline. The Federal Reserve paper factory is a house of cards. The U.S. banking system is so fragile that, according to Federal Reserve chairman Arthur Burns, even Congressional investigation runs the risk of creating panic.

The fragility is emphasized by the extraordinary proportion of bank assets comprising New York City paper. Some 546 U.S. banks include New York City securities as 20 percent or more of their assets *and 179 of these commercial banks are brave enough to hold 50 percent or more of their capital in New York City and State obligations!* If the average depositor thinks about these figures a little, it may not take a Congressional investigation to start the panic, and thus bring down the house of cards.

Even from the inside of the debt pyramid, the possibility of collapse is ever-present and the danger of bank runs a very plausible phenomena. For example, during the behind-the-scenes agonizing in the early days of the discovery of a $30 million trading loss at the United California Bank's subsidiary in Switzerland, a run on UCB was considered likely. As "Adam Smith" described one scene:

> *On Sunday, August 30, 1970, Frank King led the group of UCB officials who met [with Paul Erdman, Vice President of the United California Bank in Basel] in a conference room at the Beverly Hilton. The president of the bank, according to Paul, was philosophical. "Win some, lose some," he said. The one concern everyone seemed to have was to keep the affair secret to avoid a run on the bank. . . .**

The pressure on the inside of the pyramid is to prevent debt holders from moving from the illiquid portion of the debt pyramid to the liquid portion — and particularly to prevent debt holders from converting their intangible asset, paper, into tangible gold. One important aspect of the war on gold is to set up bar-

---

*"Adam Smith," *Supermoney*, (New York: popular Library), p. 155.

riers to the ultimate liquidity of gold: by propaganda against gold, by price-depressing techniques against gold, even by making transactions in or ownership of gold illegal.

The remaining question is not whether the debt structure *will* collapse, but *when*. What do we mean by "collapse"? H. A. Merklein defines collapse as a "combination of unemployment and inflation so rampant that the market ceases to function effectively."* Merklein suggests that, given a 50-percent inflation rate, "public confidence in government issued fiat money tends to break down . . . and barter begins to replace the money economy." According to Merklein's calculations, with a ten-percent unemployment rate, collapse could begin at 30-percent inflation — a figure exceeded by the United Kingdom, Argentina, and Italy in 1975. Even granted the existence of many unknowns, Merklein's evidence does suggest the early 1980s as Doomsday for the United States. Similar calculations by Wesley H. Hillendahl, vice president of the Bank of Hawaii, also suggests the early 1980s as the region of economic collapse.†

Of one thing we can be sure: If we continue the paper-debt money "something-for-nothing" road to a welfare state, collapse is inevitable. *Sauve qui peut!*

---

*"Can the U.S. economy collapse?" *World Oil*, December 1975.
†Wesley H. Hillendahl, *Big Government's Destruction of the American Economy*, (Connecticut: Committee for Monetary Research and Education, Inc., (July 1974), Monetary Tract, Number 4.

CHAPTER NINE
The Road to Rambouillet

A cardinal rule of international finance is, "pay more attention to what central bankers or governments do than what they say."

John Exter, former Senior Vice President of Citibank and Vice President of the Federal Reserve Bank of New York [March 1976].

KNOWLEDGE OF THE FRAGILE NATURE of the debt pyramid was one of the factors that led world financial "leaders" to examine urgently the troublesome monetary structure.

In the Fall of 1975, political leaders of the Western world met in sumptuous surroundings at Chateau Rambouillet, France. The purpose of the high-level meeting was to solve the world monetary problems they themselves had created. To judge by the results, the discussions were hardly more productive than previous meetings. The *London Economist* commented caustically:

> *We have six countries that led the world into its second worst slump and its first slumpflation declaring they will not let recovery falter, nor accept another outburst of inflation.* *

---

*November 22, 1975.

The Rambouillet meetings marked the end of the 1944 Bretton-Woods era (and the dollar supremacy), rather than the dawn of a new international monetary cooperation. Beneath this "flummery," as the *Economist* called it, reality still existed. The industrial West was in its second-worst slump of all time; but few inquired of monetary history, "What of the gold standard years preceding 1929?"*

In fact, the monetary crises of the nineteenth century, which are universally decried as unbearable by modern Keynesians, were both mild and brief (and a lot less traumatic) than the depressions of 1929-1932 and even 1974-1975. They were mild and brief for very good reasons: from 1820 to 1914 the world was on a full gold standard, and a full gold standard makes it almost impossible for politicians to break the rules of the financial game for domestic or external political purposes. Gold as we have noted before is an effective discipline.

In other words, from 1820 to 1914 the politicians could not, to any great extent, manipulate their economic system for their own advantage or that of their backers. And neither could the international bankers, to any significant degree. So "the Road to Rambouillet" began in 1914, when the world went off the gold standard and shifted onto a paper fiat standard.

The gold exchange standard adopted by 32 countries after World War I (only 12 returned to the gold standard proper) had a fatal flaw: it was not a *true* gold standard because sterling and dollar reserves were counted as reserve assets, and so presented an elastic opportunity to move away from the discipline of gold. That paper sterling and paper dollars were counted as the equivalent of gold was the fatal flaw in the gold exchange standard.

In one very real sense the Rambouillet meetings marked the end of the fiat money road, as well as the Bretton Woods agreement, because to any competent outside observer the world paper-money balloon was under attack. The world monetary system was unstable. Each country had an incentive to save itself at the expense of others.

After 1975, we find a clear division of world monetary al-

---

*One of the few was the Editor of the English Establishment's voice, the *Times* (London). See, Williams Rees-Mogg, *The Reigning Error*, (London: Hamilton Publishers, 1974).

liances. There is the paper-dollar, anti-gold forces at the International Monetary Fund, dominated by the United States (and thus the Wall Street-Rockefeller interests), on the one hand. While on the other there is the old European financial establishment (usually thought of as dominated by the Rothschild financial power), which has moved away for pragmatic reasons from the paper dollar, imposed under the Bretton Woods agreement, towards the stability of gold. This faction obviously intends to use the Bank for International Settlements as its intermediary and agent.

In 1944, Europe had no alternative to the Bretton Woods agreement; it had no gold. But thanks to U.S. defeats in the gold pool war, Europe now has ample gold reserves. Those of France, Germany, and Switzerland combined exceed the United States' stock.

In brief, Rambouillet marked the end of the U.S.-dominated IMF as an unchallenged world monetary force and the subsequent division of world financial power into two camps: a gold-oriented Europe and a paper-dollar-oriented United States.

How did this twin-pole international scene develop between 1914 and 1975? In 1914 world trade was dominated by sterling. World War I reduced the importance of sterling and Britain ended the war with heavy debts to the United States. The post-war world was dominated by two currencies — the potentially weak sterling and the potentially strong dollar. The growth and implementation of socialist ideas, political opportunism, changes in mores, and development of the "something-for-nothing" philosophy were all fertile fields to cultivate the argument that "gold is too scarce to act as a numeraire."

So for the 32 countries that adopted the gold exchange standard in the early 1920s, as we have previously noted, sterling and dollars as well as gold became reserve assets. But the fear of a "gold shortage" was a myth.* There must always be some market clearing price at which the demand for gold equals the supply of gold. In economic theory there is no such thing as a "shortage" if we allow the market mechanism to operate.

---

*This myth was promoted in numerous books and articles, and is still cited as a reason to reject gold. See, for example, The Royal Institute of International Affairs, *The International Gold Problem: Collected Papers*, (London: Oxford University Press, 1931).

What the "gold-shortage" promoters really mean is that the financial and political powers do not *want* to allow gold to act as a discipline, because those manipulators could not impose a "something-for-nothing" political system under a disciplined monetary system.

The search for an "elastic currency" to overcome the mythical gold shortage, the reluctance to submit to the discipline of the full gold standard, and several disasterous monetary episodes (such as Winston Churchill's overvaluation of sterling in the mid-1920s), plus wartime inflation and structural industrial weaknesses, led to the monetary disequilibriums of the 1920s. The United States compounded the problem with vast reparations loans to Europe — which generated vast profits for Wall Street and vast losses for the American public. Thus the "debt moratorium problem" of the early 1930s was created. France, reflecting its traditional trust in gold, absorbed gold from the rest of the world on a large scale. So the inevitable happened in 1933: the collapse of a weak bank, the Credit Anstalt in Vienna, led to monetary panic and the partial collapse of the gold exchange standard. Currencies tied to gold appreciated; the French franc rose dramatically in 1933-1934, much as the Swiss franc, backed by gold, behaves today. On the other hand, sterling, which was not heavily backed by gold, depreciated heavily in the early 1930s, just as in 1976.

By the mid-1930s the preliminary skirmishes of World War II were under way. The Spanish Civil War and the Abyssinian campaign had begun; and American technical assistance to both Nazi Germany and the Soviet Union, and the use of this technical assistance to build the Nazi war machine and the Red Army, was well underway. These profitable technical-assistance programs were the virtual monopolies of larger U.S. firms controlled by Wall Street interests. Out of World War II came the Bretton Woods agreement of 1944 and the International Monetary Fund, two systems which pegged all currencies to the U.S. dollar. The dollar alone was pegged to gold. To achieve stability in the system, permission was required for any change in exchange rates outside a narrow range, and there were a series of such upward (revaluation) and downward (devaluation) moves from 1946 into the 1960s.

In brief, from the Genoa Conference of 1922 sterling and

the U.S. dollar (then after 1944 the dollar alone) were used as "paper gold" or gold substitutes. In 1970 the United States decided to go a step further and *create* paper gold out of nothing: the so-called Special Drawing Rights, or SDRs.

A Flash of Genius: Paper Gold

One of the lessons of the gold pool fiasco was that European central bankers were not about to defend the American dollar to the last ounce of European gold. European central bankers were aware that towering overseas dollar libilities were a painless device used by the United States to extract something for nothing, to leave unwanted dollars in lieu of traditional gold transfers.

The United States, committed after 1968 to a war against gold to protect the remaining U.S. gold reserves, hit on the idea to make "something for nothing" work for *every* central banker. Once implemented, European bankers could have no complaints about the United States deficits and the pile of unwanted dollars. The scheme, officially adopted in July 1969 and launched in January 1970, was called "Special Drawing Rights."

SDRs are reserves created out of nothing, like Federal Reserve notes, allocated to members of the International Monetary Fund according to fund quota subscriptions of gold and currency. For example, in the first allocation the U.S. received 2.3 billion SDRs and Botswana 1.5 million. Initially the SDR was defined in terms of gold; one SDR equaled .889 of a gram of gold, the same definition as the 1969 dollar. Later the dollar was twice devalued, putting the SDR at a premium to the dollar. Subsequently, the SDR was defined in terms of a basket of currencies, rather than gold, as part of the program to demonetize gold.

The fundamental quality of SDRs is that they are imaginery or pretend money. They are actually computer inputs, rather than paper certificates, but are aptly named "paper gold." SDRs have no intrinsic value. In fact, they do not exist; they are phantoms. They are arbitrarily created out of nothing. They represent nothing. John Exter, former vice president of the Federal Reserve Bank of New York, calls them "I-owe-you-nothings."

The International Monetary Fund can create one million or 500 billion SDRs in ten minutes, with a brief computer instruction. They are the ultimate infinitely flexible money. And as such, they are the ultimate generators for infinite inflation.

Support for SDRs was enthusiastic in the Establishment financial community. The collective memory of international monetary experts apparently stops at the day before yesterday. Fritz Machlup, an international economics academic at Princeton University, burbled that "SDRs are becoming a new international money." He gave paper gold his "enthusiastic backing." The underdeveloped countries were not slow to recognize their "free lunch," and were understandably grateful. SDRs thus became a useful if a minor means to bail the Third World out from pressing oil bills and development costs. The Third World has become somewhat less enthusiastic as its allocations are used up, but still the underdeveloped countries recognize a gift. Even a propaganda gesture was included, when the agreement was worked out in the handsome Kenyatta Conference Center at the 1973 Nairobi meeting of the International Monetary Fund.

The End of the Bretton Woods Agreement

The creation of SDRs has undoubtedly contributed to the illusion that gold was being demonetized. The end of the first battle in the gold war (but *not* of the war against gold) came on August 15, 1971, when President Nixon suspended convertibility of paper dollar claims into gold for foreign-government holders of U.S. paper dollars. This amounted to an admission of technical bankruptcy by the United States. President Nixon did not suspend the conversion of gold claims into U.S. paper.

In theory, if gold is indeed a worthless barbaric relic, as claimed, then as it is phased out of the world monetary system we would expect to see it exchanged at a discount to U.S. paper dollars. In other words, to demonetize gold the paper dollar should be at a premium, because of the paper dollar's greater intrinsic value (or its value in exchange) with "worthless" gold. But this is the real world, not a fantasy land, and in actual practice the paper dollar was discounted — so much so that U.S.

stocks of gold could not satisfy persistent attempts to exchange paper for gold. The crisis aspect of the Gold Pool War in 1967 was repeated on May 5, 1971, when heavy dollar inflows into Europe closed the foreign exchange markets in Austria, Belgium, West Germany, Netherlands, and Switzerland.

In August 1971 there was a major "run on the bank." Foreign holders of U.S. claims wanted to exchange their paper-dollar claims for gold. The United States could not satisfy the claims and closed the gold window. It was, in effect, a declaration of bankruptcy. When President Nixon closed the gold window he did not, as he said, demonetize gold. On the contrary, he demonetized the dollar! Regardless of his words, his *actions* emphasized the premium value of gold over fiat dollars. The propaganda war on gold by the U.S. since 1971 has been designed to prevent this single fact from penetrating the consciousness of the American public. When the real significance of the demonetization of the dollar is fully grasped by Americans, the result will be monetary panic, probably followed by the collapse of the debt pyramid.

Closing the gold window was a new phenomena in American monetary history. The Continental bill had been freely convertible into gold and silver, even when it took 2,000 paper Continental bills to equal one gold dollar. Suspension of convertibility in 1971 meant that there was *no* rate at which foreign claims on the United States would be exchanged for gold. An ounce of gold was thus worth an infinite amount of paper dollars.

The European response to suspension of convertibility was to allow the U.S. dollar to find its own level in the market place without intervention, and all countries (except France) allowed their currencies to float when the exchanges reopened on August 21, 1971. In October, a meeting of finance ministers and central bankers in Rome produced the usual face-saving appeal to restore financial stability and reform the system. A year later, in December 1972, the Group of Ten met in Washington and produced the so-called Smithsonian Agreement. Under this compact, wider exchange margins were introduced and the U.S. devalued the dollar by 7.9 percent. This was the equivalent of raising the price of gold from $35 to $38 an ounce, which is hardly consistent with demonetizing gold.

By February 1972 the International Monetary Fund had sold its remaining U.S. investments and had withdrawn its gold from the Federal Reserve Bank and Bank of England vaults. In June 1972 the IMF proposed a formation of the "Committee of Twenty" to recommend a new international monetary system. In November 1972 the IMF announced its intention to finish work on this "fully reformed international monetary system" within two years (that is, by September 1974).

At the conclusion of the December 1972 discussions in Washington, President Nixon — persuaded, no doubt, that the Committee of Twenty could indeed come up with a reform package — claimed that the Smithsonian Agreement would be "The most significant monetary agreement in the history of the world. . . ." Nixon's claim collapsed just two months later, when the U.S. Government announced on February 12, 1973 its intention to mini-devalue the dollar again. The change this time would be ten percent: the equivalent of raising the price of gold from $38 to $42.22 per ounce. The subsequent wave of speculation against the dollar led to the closing of foreign exchange markets once again; they were not reopened until March 19. Both dollar devaluations focused world attention on the decline of the dollar in terms of gold, while neither devaluation recognized that the free market place price of gold in terms of U.S. dollars was far higher than $38 or $42 an ounce.

In any event, the Committee of Twenty went about its business of reforming the world monetary system. In July 1973 the Committee agreed that the new system should allow official *sales* of gold in the free market. In November this conclusion was confirmed when the central bank governors of Belgium, West Germany, Italy, the Netherlands, Switzerland, the United Kingdom, and the United States terminated the 1968 agreement which prohibited central-bank gold sales on the private market. So ended the two-tier market for gold.

But this is about as far as the Committee of Twenty got in its two-year reform program. In January 1974 the Committee decided that first, they needed much more time to reform the system; and second, priority areas should be established for immediate work.

In April 1974 the finance ministers of the European Economic Community agreed that European central banks should be able not only to sell gold but also to *buy* gold among themselves, at market-related prices, and to make these gold *purchases* on the free market at market-related prices. This move flatly opposed the U.S. claim that gold was in the process of being demonetized. Precisely the opposite was true: gold was quietly being introduced back into the monetary system by the European finance ministers and central bankers, who are not inclined to support ideological crusades where their own well-being is concerned.

On June 11, 1974 the finance ministers moved one step further toward the adoption of gold when they agreed that gold should be used as collateral for loans between central banks. This was a fundamental step, soon to be used in loans to Italy, Portugal, and Uruguay. Further, the ministers agreed, the valuation of the gold collateral was to be at market-related prices. In the first such loan, from West Germany to Italy, the collateral was valued at $120 an ounce. This established a quasi-official floor for the price of gold that was 2.8 times higher than the price set by the United States.

In December 1974 an important meeting between the Presidents of France and the United States was held on the island of Martinique in the Caribbean. It was agreed (obviously at the French request) that a government could now value its reserve gold holdings at current market prices, with an allowance for revision at six-month intervals in light of market-price changes. France promptly revalued her gold reserves to $170 an ounce. Then, on December 31, 1974, the United States removed the official ban on gold ownership by U.S. citizens. At the same time it began a massive internal propaganda campaign, with the help of an unquestioning media, against gold holding. The Treasury began its possibly illegal gold auctions* to depress the price of gold and scare off domestic purchases.

In the midst of these bear raids on the gold market, the secretive Rambouillet conference was held in November 1975 between the heads of state of West Germany, Italy, Japan, France, the United Kingdom, and the United States. The result-

---

*See Appendix A.

ing compromise between the European pro-gold and the U.S. anti-gold positions was smoothed at the subsequent IMF meeting in Jamaica. The full story of the Rambouillet discussions has not yet been revealed. It appears that at first France, later joined by Germany, pressed the United States for an international meeting to resolve outstanding questions on the new international monetary order (particularly the floating-fixed exchange rate dilemma, where the U.S. and France held diametrically opposed views), and the still-vexing gold question. When it came down to hard bargaining, France yielded on its demand for fixed exchange rates in return for U.S. concessions on gold.

Somewhere along the line, perhaps at the later 1976 Jamaica meeting, the less-developed countries pleaded for more financial assistance and the gold question got tangled up with the aid appeal. The result was an agreement that 25 million ounces of IMF gold would be auctioned off, and the funds used for aid purposes.

Revival of the Bank for International Settlements

The Bank for International Settlement was created in 1930 by the central banks of the major countries as a means of settling inter-bank accounts. The BIS, which is based in Basle, Switzerland, faded into the background after the creation of the International Monetary Fund in the 1944 Bretton Woods agreement. But in 1975 the fortunes of the pro-gold BIS revived.

At the 30th Annual Meeting of the IMF, held between Labor Day and September 5, 1975 in Washington, D.C., the Committee of Twenty hammered out an agreement generally hailed as a monetary victory. Both the "official price" of gold at $42.22 an ounce and the requirement to use gold in official IMF transactions were eliminated. Faced with deep divisions over the future role of gold, the officials finally agreed that one-sixth of the gold held by IMF on behalf of its members, or 25 million ounces, would be returned to members and that a further one-sixth would be sold, with the proceeds going to developing nations. The market place would be allowed to establish the price of gold.

Finally, the finance ministers agreed that members would be given the freedom to buy and sell gold as a reserve asset. The participants did agree that total gold holdings would not be increased, but that clause was limited to two years.

It is clear from the discussion and the agreements that there was no unanimity of agreement at the IMF meeting. The results represent a crude compromise between pro-gold and anti-gold forces. There are reports that the Bank for International Settlements put pressure on the U.S. to include the pro-gold items by threatening not to renew U.S. debts when they became due. (Since there is no way for the U.S. to repay its huge obligations, the short-term debt has to be "rolled over," or renewed, periodically.) Given the shaky debt pyramid this must have been an effective persuader. Treasury Secretary William Simon, whistling past the graveyard as usual, hailed the agreement as a *coup* for the demonetization of gold. South African Finance Minister O. P. F. Horwood told a New York meeting, "If this amounts to phasing gold out of the monetary system, let us have more of it!"

Similarly, the Jamaica meeting in 1976 was a trade-off between underdeveloped countries looking for a handout, plus some compromise for tentative changes in the role of gold and the use of exchange-rate adjustments and quotas. Billed as a final solution to the world's monetary problems, the Jamaica meeting was followed by several months of currency turmoil: the pound collapsed, followed by fall of the Italian lira, the French franc, and the Spanish peseta.

The underdeveloped countries were offered $3 billion in aid, of which some $500 million would come from the sale of IMF gold. The IMF now proposed to return another 1/6th of its stock (25 million ounces) to its members and to auction off 1/6th over a four-year period. Significantly, the Bank for International Settlements was given the right to bid at these auctions for its own account and on behalf of central banks. Profits over the official price of $42 an ounce were earmarked for the undeveloped countries. The official gold price was abolished, marking the official end of the two-tier system, and floating exchange rates were legalized. Both quotas and credit facilities were enlarged, but quotas would be paid only in domestic fiat currency.

What the Jamaica meeting did was create an opportunity for European central banks to increase their gold stocks through the Bank for International Settlements, while converting the IMF into a paper mill. South African Minister of Finance O. P. F. Horwood commented that the Jamaica meeting "in reality reaffirms and entrenches the monetary role of gold." It is worth noting that as far back as June 1971 the South African Reserve Bank subscribed to shares in the Bank for International Settlements and thus became a member. Twenty-five European central banks are members; South Africa is one of only five non-European members of the BIS.

The reshuffling of international monetary institutions was confirmed in early 1976. A new building was under construction for the BIS in Basle, and the organization acquired a new head of its monetary and economics department: Alexandre Lamfalussy, managing director and member of the executive committee of the Belgian Banque Bruxelles Lambert, which is affiliated with the Rothschild group. Lamfalussy is not perhaps as vocally pro-gold as his predecessor, Milton Gilbert; but there is no reason to believe he does not reflect the increasing pro-gold orientation of BIS members.

Almost simultaneously, Paul Volcker, formerly with Rockefeller's Chase Manhattan Bank in New York and one of the more vocal Washington paper fanatics, arrived in his new position as president of the Federal Reserve Bank of New York.

Looking back over the IMF road to Rambouillet and Jamaica, the U.S. Treasury since the early 1960s has been embarked on a campaign to retain world dollar supremacy through the IMF. The U.S. has failed. First, it failed to keep European central bankers from exchanging dollars for gold. Second, it failed to prevent reintroduction of gold into the international monetary system. And third, it failed to stop the use of the BIS as a vehicle for international exchange in competition with the International Monetary Fund.

The banking world *outside the United States* is moving towards gold, not away from it.

Whether or not the IMF is in the final stages of dissolution, as some observers state, it is obvious that the BIS has a renewed lease on life. It may well evolve into a gold-oriented European bank for central bankers.

The End of the Road Is in Sight

The division of the world monetary arena into two camps, pro-gold and anti-gold, sets the stage for the final conflict. The current battle — one the U.S. Treasury *must* win or go down in disgrace — is to prevent significant numbers of American investors from acting on the paper-gold equation. At all costs the American citizen has to be persuaded that paper dollars are at least equal to, if not better than, gold. The Treasury is embarked on a continuing anti-gold propaganda campaign; it will continue to sell gold, albeit reluctantly — perhaps even reducing its stock below the $10 billion level. And it will attempt to convince the European bankers to return to a system dependent on the U.S. paper dollar.

Coupled with its propaganda ploys and diplomatic maneuvering, there is now depressing evidence of a (hopefully limited) resort to phony statistics by the paper fanatics. For instance, the October 1975-January 1976 U.S. Government statistics on the "composite index of business indicators" shows a buoyant recovery. But in fact the figures have been quietly and without publicity revised *downwards* in each of the four months. Another example is the pressure not to publish the U.S. balance-of-payments figures, on the grounds that such figures are "meaningless and misleading." (Deficits on balance of payments are carefully watched as an indicator of possible gold-price actions.)

In brief, evidence is surfacing of a fear among government officials that the gold war may already be lost. This fear was best expressed by Deputy Treasury Secretary Jack F. Bennett during his testimony against gold legalization before the Senate Banking Committee. If Congress legalized gold ownership for U.S. citizens, said Bennett, we would be threatened with "a major catastrophe of the same magnitude as a Martian invasion or a nuclear attack."*

These paper-versus-gold battles have been fought before. The stark fact is that paper currency and debt money have *never* emerged triumphant in a straight, head-on battle with gold. Why

---

*Quoted in *Coin World*, May 30, 1973.

not? Because gold has tangible worth and is limited in supply. Paper has negligible tangible worth and is unlimited in supply. At Rambouillet and Kingston the battle lines became clear. On one side are the gold suppliers, South Africa and Russia, together with the European central bankers and a polyglot of private gold buyers, ranging from disgruntled Americans to Arab sheiks. On the other side are the U.S. Treasury, Wall Street bankers, and the U.S. Establishment, plus a sinking Britain. The latter has one major advantage: it is in command of a sophisticated propaganda machine. But history universally supports the former.

While the European central bankers wanted all IMF gold returned to its claimants, the U.S. wanted all IMF gold dumped onto the free market, to depress the price. Then a third force emerged, the third world of underdeveloped countries, demanding the proceeds from IMF gold sales as a free gift to offset their chronic balance-of-payments problems. These underdeveloped countries want IMF sales at a maximum price, to generate maximum revenues, of course. But this conflicts with the U.S. need to dump gold to *depress* the price. And the United States can hardly pose now as an enemy of the underprivileged nations.

After Rambouillet, the U.S. was almost alone, apart from an economically impotent Britain, fighting a battle to reduce the role of gold, while the rest of the world was quietly and deliberately moving to restore gold to its role as a key reserve asset.

After the Rambouillet and Jamaica Conferences, the U.S. Treasury cranked out its typical wishful thinking and anti-gold propaganda. Secretary Simon boasted, "We achieved the ultimate monetary reform that we all came to accomplish." Britain's Chancellor of the Exchequer, Denis Healey, dutifully echoed, "We have unanimously agreed that gold should be phased out of the IMF system." Jamaica was followed by a run on the pound, a run on the lira and suspension of the Italian foreign exchange market, a run on the French franc, and a ten-percent devaluation of the Spanish peseta. All these followed within a few weeks of Simon's announcement of "the ultimate monetary reform."

To bring the U.S. actions at Chateau Rambouillet and Kingston, Jamaica into focus, and incidentally to view these actions as European bankers do, let us assume that the reader decides to imitate the U.S. Treasury in handling his personal monetary af-

fairs. It would work something like this, following the same sequence we have just described for the U.S. Government:

First, acquire debts of a million or so, by running up charge
accounts, borrowing from banks, getting personal loans from
friends, or whatever. Just spend, spend, spend, and then borrow, borrow, borrow, so you can spend some more. When there
are more bills than money in the bank, keep adding to the debt
pile until bills are ten times greater than your liquid assets (that
is, you owe ten times more than all of your cash and all of the
goods you own that can be quickly converted into cash).

Next, make a public announcement: admit that your debts
are ten times greater than your assets, but declare that it
doesn't really matter *because these debts are now worthless*. In
the future, so goes your unilateral declaration, the only acceptable currency for repayment of your debts will be "Smiths" or
"Browns," or whatever the newly printed paper notes you will
issue are to be called.

Third, make another declaration. State that your creditors'
money is worthless; call their currency "merely outdated barbaric relics;" announce that herewith and henceforth they are
demonetized. From here on the only valid acceptable currency
will be "Smiths" and "Browns."

What would happen to any reader who attempted such a
stunt? Presumably, if he managed to avoid the men in white
coats, there would be mocking publicity, followed by a sober
and severe day in court. Regrettably, there is no body of law and
no court that can indict the Treasury officials and politicians
who use the police power of the State to make similar declar-
ations and to implement such policies on a national scale.

The Treasury, the Federal Reserve System, and the Congress are under the illusion that they can decree what is money.
They cannot. They can legislate legal tender, but that is not
necessarily the same thing. Money is what people and countries
will accept in exchange for goods and services. This may, or may
not, be paper dollars. Historically, as we have seen, money has
been gold, silver, copper, and even iron. These currencies have
led to stable monetary systems. Money has also been leather,
mulberry leaves, and rice paper; today it is wood pulp and ink
and the present debt system. Historically, the latter have been
the unstable systems. Why? Because at some point holders of

these latter moneys look for something of intrinsic value as a store of wealth, and they find none. The search for something of intrinsic value to use as money can be identified in recent times. It was soap and cigarettes in Germany in 1946; it was gold taels in South Vietnam in 1975. When disaster strikes, and confidence is shattered or government credibility is breached, then citizens turn to a currency with intrinsic value. And they will ignore whatever device the government or the bureaucracy may decree.

Oddly enough, it is government itself that provides much of the ammunition to destroy public confidence in the monetary system. Today, almost any issue of any financial newspaper contains numerous examples of such evidence. For example, one issue of the *Wall Street Journal*, selected at random, reported on April 30, 1976 that: (1) more than 90 employees of the IMF earn larger salaries than the U.S. Secretary of the Treasury, but were complaining because their 1976 increases were limited to 5.8 percent; (2) a number of Congressmen have filed "false travel expenses" — a felony — and had the gall to admit they did so, sure they would face, at the worst, a mild rebuke; (3) there were enough reports of price increases to make nonsense out of the government's assertion that inflation is under control at two percent; and (4) a Gallup Poll on behalf of the American Bankers Association proudly announced that 93 percent (up from 90 percent last year) of "those interviewed" thought their bank deposits were "very safe" or "fairly safe." (The article did not comment on what actions the ten percent or seven percent who were concerned about the safety of their deposits were taking.)

A steady flow of news of this type (and this was one day, picked at random), cumulatively will undermine confidence. It does not require a series of major news stories announcing the cataclysm to break public confidence; a slow accumulation of smaller items and events will accomplish the same thing.

The Treasury dilemma is compounded because, although Treasury officials may see the nature of the problem they have on their hands, they are bound by ideological ropes to collectivist ideals. As a result, they resort to blindfold tactics. For example, in the face of a $100 billion Eurodollar debt, Treasury Secretary Simon related to a Congressional committee that there is no "overhang" of dollars held involuntarily by foreigners.

Said Simon, "Who is it that is trying to dispose of unwanted dollars? I am unable to find them." The Congressional Subcommittee on International Trade quickly picked up the theme and declared:

> *Private foreigners are in no way constrained to hold dollars. To the extent that they do they must be presumed to be acting in their best interest.**

These statements were made in 1975. Four years earlier, the United States had suspended convertibility of dollars into gold. After 1971 foreigners had no opportunity to dispose of their dollars, except in exchange for other paper dollars. When the debts were originally contracted the foreign claimants expected payment in gold, if they wished. But the gold window was slammed in 1971. Now they are offered either U.S. dollars or U.S. dollars, not U.S. dollars or gold. Naturally Simon cannot find anyone wanting to dispose of dollars. In terms of our earlier analogy, it is as if the reader with his pile of bills payable only in "Smiths" and "Browns" shuts his eyes and says, "Who is it that is trying to collect bills in dollars? I am unable to find them."

The acid test is what would happen if the U.S. announced the dollar was today freely convertible into gold. *Then* Secretary Simon and Congress would see who wants to hold dollars, and who wants to hold gold. Back in 1810, when the British Bullion Committee was wrestling with the problem of restoring gold convertibility for sterling, it waited almost a decade. It stocked up the Bank of England vaults with more gold than outstanding paper claims before announcing convertibility of the paper pound.

To restore dollar convertibility today, without triggering a stampede on the Treasury, the U.S. needs a minimum $100 billion of gold in its vaults; it has only $12 billion (at the old official price of $35 an ounce). Of course, the alternative is to allow the price of gold to rise — but as we have seen that is what the war on gold is all about.

---

*U.S. House of Representatives, *Exchange Rate Policy and International Monetary Reform*, Report of the Subcommittee on International Trade, Investment and Monetary Policy, (Washington, D.C.: 1975).

To appreciate that the end of the road is now in sight, it is important to remember the significance of dollar-gold convertibility. When currencies are freely convertible, anyone can interchange currencies at will at the prevailing market rates. Thus, a freely convertible dollar means that dollars can always be exchanged into gold — and conversely that gold can always be converted into dollars. When conversion is suspended, it means that the currency can no longer be exchanged for gold. The option still remains, if anyone wants to use it, of exchanging gold for paper dollars.

If the dollar is not convertible into gold — in other words, if its convertibility is suspended — the significant attribute is that dollar holders can no longer obtain gold. On the other hand, gold holders can obtain dollars. In short, it is the convertibility of the dollar that is suspended, not the convertibility of gold. The bankrupt debtor is the U.S., which can only pay in paper dollars or "paper gold," not physical gold. The solvent creditors are the holders of gold and claims on gold. The Treasury Department's propaganda not withstanding, it is the U.S. dollar that has been demonetized since 1971, not gold.

Now if the U.S. Treasury wanted to demonetize gold in a meaningful way, one that has reason and substance and will prevail over time, then suspending the convertibility of the dollar is not the way to do it. The Treasury must try to suspend the convertibility of gold. What has happened in practice is that in 1971 the U.S. suspended convertibility of the dollar into gold and simultaneously claimed that gold was being phased out of the monetary system. This is Alice in Wonderland nonsense. The key question is: can the U.S. pay its debts in gold as required by claims held abroad? The answer is an unequivocal *no*! Consequently, the U.S. is technically bankrupt; gold is already the winner.

What the 1975 Rambouillet and 1976 Jamaica meetings achieved was to convince the European central bankers that the U.S. Treasury had no intention of surrendering its Alice in Wonderland dream about the supremacy of the paper dollar in the new international world order. Whether the world knows it yet or not, the world monetary system is now divided into two camps: a U.S.-dominated International Monetary Fund devoted to the maintenance of paper-dollar supremacy, or dollar imperialism, and a European-dominated Bank for International Settlements devoted to fixed exchange rates tied to the tried-and-tested anchor of gold.

At the end of the road, a worthless paper dollar will be rejected; a secure gold dollar will be triumphant.

CHAPTER TEN
The New Gold Market

The paper dollar has become an "IOU nothing,"
as have all paper currencies in the world today. As
such, one "IOU nothing" currency has to trade in the
marketplace every minute of every day against the
"IOU nothings" of all the other central banks. We are
in a world of irredeemable paper money — a state of af-
fairs unprecedented in history.

John Exter, former vice president of the Federal Reserve Bank of New York.

THE DECADES-LONG HISTORY of the modern paper-money spree
came to an end in one very real sense in the fall of 1975. The
Chateau Rambouillet Conference reestablished the role of gold
in the world monetary order; the decision was confirmed at the
IMF Jamaica meeting the following January. The newly emerging Bank for International Settlements (BIS) will act as an agent
for European central banks and a few non-European countries,
while the IMF will degenerate into an engine of inflation to
grant soft loans and easy money to third world countries.

When the Rambouillet conferees agreed to the sale of IMF
gold, they not only completed division of the world into anti-
gold and pro-gold camps, but at the same time they introduced

mechanisms for the use of gold as collateral for international loans and as a central-bank reserve asset. What will this reintroduction of gold into world monetary affairs do to the market for gold in the coming decades? In this chapter we will look first at the supply side for gold, and then at the demand side, particularly those long-range factors affecting the gold market. Attention is given to the "overhang" from the U.S. Treasury and the IMF, which are designed to create and will continue to create uncertainty as a bear tactic to depress the price. Finally, we will look at the probable outcome for gold in this new market place.

The Supply of Gold

SOUTH AFRICA: Two-thirds of the world's gold comes from a single source — a 300-mile semicircle running east and west from Johannesburg in South Africa. This persistent but difficult-to-mine auriferous belt was discovered in 1886 and developed over the past century with a great deal of technical sophistication. South Africans have pioneered in the world's most advanced deep-mining technology, simply because this enormously rich, if geologically freakish, treasure chest lies between two and three miles below the surface. The gold deposits of Australia, Canada, and elsewhere do not have the remarkable persistence of the South African deposits. As a further incentive, in many South African mines uranium (now worth up to $40 per pound of U-308) is also an important byproduct. There are no geological or technical developments on the horizon to change this supply picture in any fundamental way.

World gold production has increased from six-million ounces per year in 1870 to about 40-million ounces in 1974. The paramount role of South Africa in total gold production is suggested by the chart on page 167.

THE SOVIET UNION: The U.S.S.R. provides about 420 metric tons of gold a year (eight times more than the United States), or about 28 percent or so of total world output. The Soviets are steadily increasing both their absolute production of gold and their share of the world market. The necessity for gold to purchase foreign technology was recognized as long ago as 1920 by Lenin; gold has since comprised an important sector of Soviet

CHART 10-1: WORLD GOLD SUPPLY (1974)
(Total 1,454.0 metric tons = 100.0 percent)

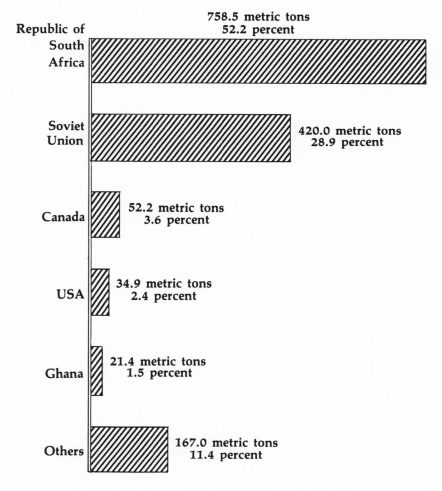

Republic of South Africa
758.5 metric tons
52.2 percent

Soviet Union
420.0 metric tons
28.9 percent

Canada
52.2 metric tons
3.6 percent

USA
34.9 metric tons
2.4 percent

Ghana
21.4 metric tons
1.5 percent

Others
167.0 metric tons
11.4 percent

Source: GOLD 1975, Consolidated Gold Fields Limited, p. 15.

foreign monetary dealings.* Taking a leaf out of the capitalist notebook, and with a healthy respect for monetary history, the Soviet Union is a vociferous gold bug and considers gold the cornerstone of a word monetary system. This realism is understandable. Who will accept inconvertible paper rubles? (As the United States must begin to ask, who is going to accept inconvertible paper dollars?)

Copying the successful marketing of the South African Krugerrand, the Soviets in 1975 reissued the 1923 chervonetz, a ten-ruble piece containing .2489 troy ounces of fine gold. The 1975 reissue was identical, except for the date and the mint initials, to the original 1923 issue, including an inscription with the slogan, "workers of the world unite." The initial mintage of 250,000 coins was sold to the world market, including 50,000 to buyers in the United States and 50,000 to Western Europe. The sales price was a hefty premium over the intrinsic gold value. The chervonetz is legal tender within the Soviet Union, although Soviet citizens are forbidden to own it — or any gold currency. But the quick international acceptance of the chervonetz is yet another signal that gold has been reintroduced as a monetary medium, while paper currencies become more and more unstable.

No fundamental change in the Soviet approach to gold can be visualized. There is a 50-year history of Soviet purchases of foreign technology to sustain a stagnant socialist economy, and periodic famines that require gold sales to offset grain purchases. The propaganda explanation for the continued Soviet grain failures (that repeated poor harvests are due to repeated adverse climatic conditions) is not acceptable. In 1900 Russia was the world's biggest grower and exporter of grain. It is the Soviets' repressive system, with its rigidly planned economy, that accounts for the grain failures, and hence Russian gold sales to generate foreign exchange to buy grain will continue as long as the planned economic system continues. However, a substantial portion of recent Soviet grain purchases have been placed in long-term storage. This may affect future grain purchases, and hence gold sales. The importance for the gold market is that

---

*See Appendix B.

Soviet sales are a depressing factor on price. It is this consideration that led South Africa's Dr. Diederichs to comment recently, "Let us hope that the Russians — although we really cannot count them among our friends — will have a good grain harvest next year."*

Dr. Diederich's realistic attitude to the Soviet Union is not shared by American Big Business, whose leaders prefer to fawn over Russian Communists in their eagerness for profitable orders. Witness Donald Kendall, chairman of Pepsi Cola, who recently attended a Kremlin dinner at which Brezhnev spoke and, presumably without choking over his vodka, gushed how fortunate he and his fellow Americans had been "to experience the great charm of this outstanding figure in the modern world." Kendall also expressed his "enormous trust" in Communist Party chieftan Bzezhnev.

In icy contrast to Kendall's Pepsi-induced mirage, on December 21, 1976, the Soviet Narodny Bank dumped one-half-billion United States dollars onto the Zurich market, requiring vigorous intervention from New York to stabilize the dollar.† This market action highlights the greatest unknown factor in the market place for the coming decade — how and when the Soviets will implement their plan for financial warfare on the United States. This plan is now in its early stages, with Soviet pressure on third world countries to default on their Western debts, but has not yet reached the stage of using Soviet gold reserves. The role of the Soviets is the key unknown for the decade of the 1980s.

The Demand for Gold

Historically, the demand for gold has been a demand for the monetary use of gold. Industrial and ornamental use of gold accounts for only a tiny fraction of recent gold purchases. Gold has been absorbed primarily by government mints and central banks as a reserve asset and for coinage. Even in the heyday of

---

Evening Post (Port Elizabeth, South Africa), October 29, 1975.
†*The Review of the News*, January 19, 1977.

CHART 10-2: MARKET BALANCE FOR GOLD: TOTAL WORLD SUPPLIES/PRIVATE PURCHASES
1956-1975 (IN METRIC TONS)

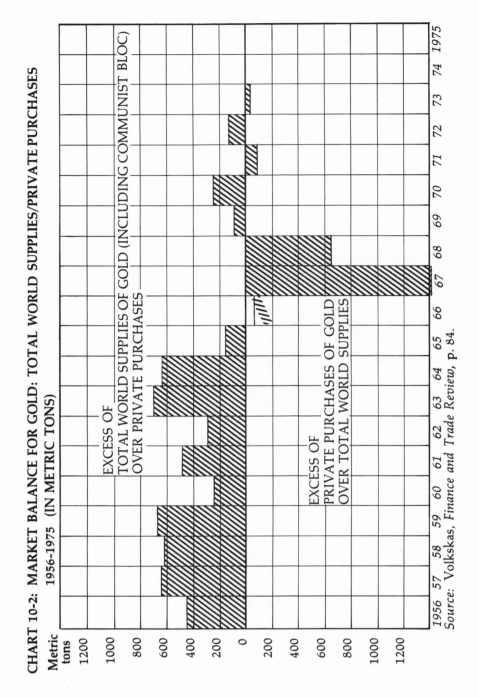

Source: Volkskas, Finance and Trade Review, p. 84.

paper-fiat currencies, central banks have continued to buy gold at the official price of $35 an ounce. The war on gold is aimed in part at removing this segment of the market. As the war has progressed, the market for gold has become progressively thinner (that is, with fewer buyers and sellers). But there are many strong indicators this will not remain the case for long.

It is highly significant for future demand that panic conditions create extraordinary gold offtakes into the private sector. Chart 10-2 demonstrates the private purchases of gold in comparison to total world supplies. It is significant that in five of the past ten years, there was a *net* movement of gold from public (*i.e.*, government) reserves to private holdings. The 2,500-metric ton offtake between October 1967 and March 1968 is especially noteworthy, especially when it is compared to the combined U.S. and IMF stock of 12,000 tons. On just *one day*, March 14, 1968, the private offtake was 400 tons, or about twice the annual U.S. industrial consumption of gold.

During 1975 there was a dramatic, if still partly hidden, turnaround in the gold picture. Public attention was concentrated on the U.S./IMF war on gold; but the reactivation of the BIS, the declared interest of European central banks in gold, and the general currency instability all suggested that, far from being demonetized, gold is in reality on the way back in as the numeraire.

Such a possibility has been noted, with alarm, by the U.S. Congress. The Joint Senate-House Subcommittee on International Economics, through its chairman Congressman Henry R. Reuss, viewed with dismay the Rambouillet proposal to restitute gold to IMF member nations. Reuss expressed concern that this move would strengthen gold in the world monetary system:

> *Equally important as the inequity of the restitution provision is the tendency it would have to accentuate rather than diminish the monetary role of gold. Gold held in the coffers of the IMF is largely immobile. But once it is returned to national central banks, gold could well be more widely used in international settlements than it is today. Moreover, if central banks value their restituted gold at market-related*

prices, the need for future SDR allocations will be reduced.*

In general, the demand for gold is still a non-U.S. demand from European central banks, institutional buyers, and private investors. For example, the Rothschild Investment Trust, Ltd. of London has an entry in its 1975 Annual Report that could not be found in any American-based mutual or investment fund. Under current assets in its 1975 report, Rothschild lists "Gold coins" with a market value of over $10 million. This was nearly one-third of the total current assets of the Rothschild Investment Trust as of March 31, 1975.

The greater part of South African gold output is marketed through Zurich, Switzerland — although the London gold fix is taken as the world price monitor. During 1975 a significant change in the marketing of South African gold occurred, reflecting a change in demand patterns that holds strong portent for the future. In early 1975 only about ten percent of South Africa's gold output was used to mint the Krugerrand, the one-ounce coin that is held mostly by individuals, not central banks, as a hedge against inflation. By the end of 1975, 25 percent of the South African gold production entered the Krugerrand presses. As a result, significantly less gold reached the world bullion market. Test marketing promotion of the Krugerrand in Philadelphia, Houston, and Los Angeles had "staggering" and "incredible" results, according to coin dealers. A major New York advertising agency, Doyle, Dane, and Bernback, was hired by the Krugerrand distributor, Intergold, to promote gold coins directly to the American public, which previously had been exposed solely to the bear-market tactics of the U.S. Government. The response was truly "staggering." By the end of 1975, Krugerrand sales were running at the rate of 5,000,000 coins annually — an amount equal almost exactly to the total proposed IMF annual sale for 1976.

It was the enormous private demand for gold as a hedge against inflation that characterized the market of the late 1960s

---

*Congress of the United States, Joint Economic Committee press release, December 18, 1975.

and was a major factor in the Gold Pool crisis of 1967. In the period 1945-1956, central banks were able to acquire almost one-half of the newly mined gold coming into the market. In the years 1960-1966, central banks and monetary authorities obtained only 26 percent; in 1967 and 1968 the gold pool operators had to *sell* 2,500 (the equivalent of two years' new production) to keep the free-market price down to the official price.*

The U.S. Treasury notwithstanding, there has been a change in the attitudes of some major countries formerly unenthusiastic about gold, especially since the 1973-1974 inflationary surge. Dr. Diederichs has noted that Italy, previously strongly anti-gold, now realizes that gold can be used as collateral for loans not obtainable by any other means. In other countries, Brazil for instance, there has been a dramatic surge in the industrial use of gold; in 1968 Brazil used only $3 million worth of gold, but by 1975 Brazilian industry used gold amounting to $237 million. This rate of consumption requires annual imports (over internal gold production) of about 50 tons.

As the London Gold Pool fell apart in 1967, two divergent roads for international monetary policy became more apparent. First, the U.S. intensified its efforts to demonetize gold. But after the Gold Pool era, these efforts were more clearly a struggle to preserve the dollar as the world's key currency. Second, other countries, initially the major European powers, and later a few of the Arab oil producers, began a search for an alternative to what they saw as dollar hegemony. The Communist states of course continued an internal policy of fiat paper money ruthlessly enforced by the State, but with a pragmatic and sophisticated use of gold in external dealings, and so must be counted in the pro-gold camp.

The two-tier system proposed by Guido Carli in 1967 was supported by the U.S. Treasury, because central banks could exchange gold at the low "official" price and by agreement would not intervene to purchase gold on the private London market or the Zurich market. But the private offtake in 1966, 1967, and 1968 exceeded all of the newly mined world supplies for those years. There were no net increases in the central bank holdings

Focus on Key Economic Issues: Gold, (University of Pretoria, November 1973), p. 1.

during those years. If the central banks had entered the private sector of the two-tier gold market as buyers, the price would have gone through the ceiling. Thus, while the U.S. Treasury had limited the use of gold by the two-tier agreement, it had not extinguished the use of gold, nor the latent demand for that "barbaric relic." For a while the anti-gold forces ignored the second tier, hoping that new supplies from Russia and South Africa would overwhelm the demand by private buyers and thus depress the price for gold. Such hopes, predictably, were in vain.

There is some question as to how much the central banks themselves honored the two-tier agreement. We noted in Chapter Seven that in the decade of 1960 to 1970, all central banks, except those of the United States, the United Kingdom, and Denmark, increased their gold holdings. This was a *net* increase, after deducting losses in the gold pool operations. Presumably either the European countries withdrew from the gold pool while their stocks were at a higher level than in 1960, or they acquired gold by some other means in the interim. In any event, the Treasury assumption was that the private market in the two-tier system could not absorb all new gold, even given the heavy net private offtake of 1966, 1967, and 1968. Thus, the price of gold would be depressed or at the worst remain in the area of the official price, with some minor risk that the two-tier system might act as a price "floor."

The single most important, long-run influence on the demand for gold is public confidence in the world's monetary systems and the worth of fiat money as a medium of exchange and a store of value. If this confidence erodes because a paper-money system cannot maintain a store of value, then paper-money holders exchange their paper for gold or other tangible assets. If paper money is *refused* as a medium of exchange, as occurred for example in Germany in 1946, then trade in commodities and a barter system are substituted. Given the high value-to-weight ratio of gold, it is less likely that gold coins will be commonly used as a day-by-day medium of exchange. (Although in the nineteenth century, it was the rule rather than the exception to pay wages in gold sovereigns, napoleons, or dollars.)

The long-run factors influencing the price of gold are relatively fixed: the small increments of new supplies come onto the market in known quantities, while the amount of newly printed paper money and debt creation is virtually unlimited and comes onto the market at the whim of governments. Thus the ratio between gold and paper constantly shifts in the direction of greater amounts of circulating paper in relation to a relatively fixed amount of gold.

Perhaps another long-run factor of potential influence on the price of gold is a broadening awareness that the argument of "insufficient gold for monetary backing" is ridiculous, and reveals a kindergarten-level of economic knowledge. By the same argument, one can say there are insufficient Cadillacs in the world (if the price of Cadillacs were made $100 each by government edict) or insufficient yachts (if the price of yachts were pegged at $500 each). There is too little gold available to supply all potential demand, if gold is priced at $35 or even $42 an ounce. The market clearing price for gold at the time of writing is between $120 and $140 an ounce. What would be the market clearing price if we required 100-percent gold backing for paper notes? In other words, what would happen if the U.S. Treasury guaranteed that every paper fiat note could be fully redeemed on demand in gold? Richard A. Marker calculates making the U.S. dollar fully redeemable would require a gold price of $1,500 an ounce. For all world currencies to be fully backed requires a gold price of about $5,800 per ounce.*

Finally, another potential influence on the long-range price of gold is the size and disposition of the overseas dollar overhang — the unwanted United States dollars and Eurodollars that are floating around the world or are being held by central banks and other institutions. One reasonable estimate of its size was presented to a congressional committee by Renaldo Levy, vice president of Marine Midland Bank of New York (one of the "problem banks" on the 1974 "watch list"):

> I would consider as real overhang any involuntary balances kept by central banking authorities both in OPEC and industrialized nations. I would guess that

---

*Richard A. Marker, *The IMF-Engine of Inflation*, (Tarzana, California: Forecaster Publishing Co., 1975).

this overhang might be in the neighbourhood of $50 to $75 billion. *

But before the same Congressional committee, Treasury Secretary Simon buried his head in the sand on the question of the "unwanted" dollar overhang and exclaimed to the Committee members: "Who is it that is trying to dispose of unwanted dollars? I am unable to find them." †

However, if holders of short-term claims decide to call for $50 to $75-billion in gold, then gold would crash through the $1,000-an-ounce barrier without pausing for breath. This is an excellent reason why the Treasury is attempting to demonetize gold. Unfortunately for the long-term welfare of the United States, American policy-makers have convinced themselves that *because* the Washington economic-political establishment has decided to write off gold as a monetary asset, everyone else in the world will be happy to go along. But everyone else most emphatically is not. For good and valid historical reasons, other countries respect the disciplinary attribute uniquely preserved in gold, or at least recognize the inevitable triumph of gold and plan accordingly.

The U.S. Treasury as a Bear Operator

The most important short-run factor affecting the gold market of the late 70s and early 80s will be sales by the U.S. and the International Monetary Fund.

After the U.S. Treasury bureaucrats decided that gold was to be demonetized and removed forever from the international monetary system, Washington was left with the not inconsequential problem of how to make its ideological decision stick. Even if money managers are ignorant of the lessons of monetary history, such as the South Sea Bubble, the English 1810 Bullion Report, the French assignats, the Continentals, the

---

*U.S. House of Representatives, *Exchange Rate Policy and International Monetary Reform*, Report of the Subcommittee on International Trade, Investment and Monetary Policy, (Washington, D.C., 1975).

†*Ibid.*, p. 137.

Greenbacks, and the centuries-old battle of fiat paper money versus gold, they are at least aware that a mere Treasury decree is unlikely to panic private gold buyers into dumping their gold holdings and promising to sin no more.

What did the Treasury do?

The gold market needed a "downer." The private buyer investing in gold as an inflation hedge needed to be discouraged. Central bankers were out of the market; all new mine output had been absorbed in 1967 by private buyers on a rising market. The logical consequence of demonetization of gold — dumping all U.S. gold stocks on the market — was and is impossible. Even the most fanatical anti-gold Treasury official is unwilling to stick his neck out *that* far. The policy that was privately adopted (but officially denied) was to dampen the gold market with *minor* periodic gold sales, accompanied by a maximum volume and amount of bearish clamor and propaganda. In other words, the U.S. Treasury is attempting to create a permanent bear atmosphere in the gold market.

Now, the U.S. Government cannot openly declare itself to be the bear operator in the market place. Officially any concerted action to depress the price of gold is denied. Among many other considerations, certain legal complications arise if any U.S. gold being sold were not auctioned off to the highest bidder — a standard requirement of the General Services Administration for the sale of any surplus government property.* But while an anti-gold, bear-market plan is officially denied, the truth has been admitted off the record by a Treasury aide:

> *You have to go through with the sale to show gold is demonetized. You have to put your money where your mouth is. The U.S. is selling gold to show that it doesn't hurt us, that it's good for us, even that we enjoy it.* †

The demagogic implications of this statement are breathtaking. It is not a policy of what is best for the American people,

---

*See Appendix A for legal arguments on this point.
† *U.S. News and World Report*, July 14, 1975.

the taxpayers, you understand. It is a matter of what is best for the Government, to support an ideological stance adopted by Treasury officials under who-knows-what outside pressures. "We're not saying it's right, or smart, or even honest," the Treasury aide seems to be saying. "We *have* to do it, so we'll put the best possible face on it."

In any event, the first Treasury sale of two million ounces of gold was scheduled for January 1975 — not so coincidentally, the very month that "legalization" of gold ownership for American citizens was once again permitted. The Treasury conducted the auction in a way that seemed planned to *minimize* returns, rather than realize the maximum price for the gold. The Treasury advertised for tenders, and these bids ranged from $1 an ounce to $185 an ounce. It then accepted only about 100 out of 219 tenders; all bids over an arbitrary $153 an ounce were accepted, those who bid less were rejected. As gold was selling at $168 per ounce on the London market, the Treasury sale had a depressing effect on the London price. But the Treasury actually cleared only 750,000 ounces, or less than one-half of the two-million ounces offered.

TABLE 10-1: FOREIGN BUYERS OF U.S. TREASURY GOLD

January 8, 1975 Sale

FOREIGN BUYER	AMOUNT (fine troy ounces)	PAID (U.S. $ per oz.)
Swiss Credit Bank	57,000	$160.00-$173.50
Dresdner Bank	387,600	$157.00-$174.00
N. M. Rothschild & Sons	15,000	$169.00-$172.00
Swiss Bank Corp	40,000	$172.50
Sharps, Pixley Inc.	41,600	$157.11-$167.50
Macotta Metals Corp	7,200	$167.78-$168.28

Total foreign sales: 548,400 ozs.
Total sold: 754,000 ozs.
Average: $165.67
Percent to foreign bidders: 70.0

June 30, 1975 Sale

FOREIGN BUYER	AMOUNT (fine troy ounces)	PAID (U.S. $ per oz.)
Swiss Credit Bank	4,000	$165.05
Campagnie de Banque et d Investissements	29,750	$165.05
N. M. Rothschild & Sons	75,750	$165.05
Swiss Bank Corp	140,000	$165.05
Johnson Mathey Bankers Ltd	6,250	$165.05
Samuel Montague & Co. Ltd	8,000	$165.05
Sharps, Pixley Inc.	58,750	$165.05
Macotta Metals Corp	32,500	$165.05
Bank of Nova Scotia	10,000	$165.05

Total foreign sales: 365,000 ozs.
Total sold: 499,500 ozs.
Average: $165.05

Percent to foreign bidders: 73.0

To maximize profits to the Treasury, as required by law, the Treasury should have instructed General Services Administration to conduct frequent sales of small amounts, with a cutoff fairly close to, *but below*, the prevailing market price. A genuine seller "puffs" his product a little; he does not tell his customers how worthless it is. On the other hand, if a seller comes into any market with large quantities, accepts only half the bids, holds the sale in a dingy backyard Washington warehouse, and makes a clamor that his product is a meaningless barbaric relic — then he is a bear operator. When the auction was completed, Treasury Secretary Simon announced himself as satisfied and commented, "The American people are a good deal smarter than some people give them credit for." He added that he did not think Americans would buy gold as an inflation hedge.

As we have noted, the Treasury gold sales had an expected depressing effect on the London gold market. Before the auction the market was steady with a morning fixing of $173 an ounce. In later trading, after results of the Treasury auction became known, gold dropped $7.50 an ounce, to about $168. One London dealer commented, "It was a very orderly market until the Americans came in. Then it was strictly one-way business with a flood of sell orders."

The plunging market is attributable to the Treasury bear approach rather than the quantity sold; 750,000 ounces is slightly more than one-half of a single day's sales. Also, the impact of the Treasury sale was on the private market for gold; European central banks had agreed not to purchase or participate. Most of the gold was purchased by private European banks and bullion firms: 70 percent of the January sale and 73 percent of the June sale went to Europeans. The Swiss Credit Bank bought 57,000 ounces in January and 4,000 ounces in June; the Swiss Bank Corporation bought 40,000 ounces in January and 140,000 ounces in June.

Taken as a percentage of annual supplies on the gold market, the Treasury quantities were minute. The price-depressant effect, therefore, was due to an irrational response to the bearish clamor set up by U.S. Government.

The combined January and June 1975 Treasury sales totalled 1,253,500 ounces, or just over 46 tons. Compared to the total of 1,500 tons of gold being mined each year, this is negligible. If such sales are repeated, then in time the price-depressing impact will diminish and the U.S. Treasury will become just another seller — albeit a noisy seller, more characteristic of a racetrack tout. The Treasury plan obviously is to maximize uncertainty in the market to depress price, and it cannot maximize uncertainty by regular sales. It can do so only by random sporadic actions at critical market turns, for example in deflationary periods accompanied by maximum propaganda.

The gold-stock overhang, equal to about 12 years of South Africa's annual supplies, is the major Treasury weapon. The Treasury cannot sell the whole of Fort Knox; even the most fanatic of the anti-gold plotters in the Treasury are unlikely to strip the U.S. of all its hard assets. So it is market anticipation or fear of massive sales that is the Treasury bear weapon, rather than the size of the sales themselves. Further, as we observed in Chapter Seven, the remaining stocks are mainly "coin melt" of .900 purity, not the "good delivery" bars normally traded on the London and Zurich markets. This is another reason why the daily London prices and the Treasury auction prices are not comparable.

While the overhang can be used as a psychological threat for a while, some kind of learning curve, or "dampened response curve," will come into play at some juncture. After half-a-dozen such price-depressing sales, a predictable pattern will emerge; the Treasury tactics will be discounted in the market place; and ultimately the Treasury sales will be greeted with yawns and the attitude that, "Ho, hum. The boys in the Treasury are at it again."

The first Treasury gold sale, in January 1975, pushed the gold price down $7.50 an ounce; the second sale, six months later, caused hardly a ripple in the market place. In brief, unless the Treasury begins dumping *tons* of gold every week, and keeps up the pressure for months, it cannot possibly force the price of gold down to the old "official" levels. In fact, if we continue to have a double-digit inflation, or another oil embargo or some other major international crisis occurs, the U.S. may not be able to dampen the price at all. Even in a place with traditionally short memories, such as the U.S. Treasury, there must be officials who remember the 1968 gold pool, when 400 tons of gold were absorbed by private buyers in a single day. That lesson has not been completely forgotten, you can be sure.

The U.S.-dominated International Monetary Fund is also intent on disposing of its gold stocks. It is making its preparations in an unusually sluggish manner, again no doubt to maximize uncertainty. The scheduled return and sale of members' gold is as follows:

Return to member countries in exchanges for currencies	25 million ounces
Donate to underdeveloped countries (in the form of gold)	7½ million ounces
To be auctioned over four years	17½ million ounces
Exchange for interest-bearing securities of IMF member-governments	100 million ounces
TOTAL	150 million ounces

The third world countries are protesting that they would prefer to receive gold, rather than the proceeds in currency from gold sales. Their argument is that gold can be used as collateral for loans, as other countries have demonstrated. They are suitably unimpressed by the U.S. argument that this approach would only reintroduce gold into the world monetary system.

Out of 150 million ounces of gold in IMF stocks, only 17½-million ounces, or 11.7 percent of the total, will come onto the open market. Most of this will be sold at monthly auctions over the next four years, but the Bank for International Settlements will probably purchase most of it on behalf of European central banks. To mitigate the depressant effects of this sale, in March 1976 South Africa sold five million ounces of gold to Swiss banks, in exchange for a package of foreign currencies. South Africa also agreed to buy back the same amount in the gold-futures market in three months (with an option to "roll over" the agreement). The remaining 100 million ounces will never see the open market. According to reports as this book goes to press, it will be exchanged for government paper securities. (How wonderful to be able to print more paper securities and exchange them for gold!)

In sum, it is obvious that the United States, directly or indirectly, has been a major factor in the pricing of gold during 1974 - 1976. Without question there will be continuing U.S. government attempts to "bear" the market. In the long run, such a policy of bearing is doomed to fail, as others have found out in the 5,000-year history of gold.

The Outcome in the Market Place

The short-run factors that cause either a rise or fall in the market price of gold are described, in great detail and with considerable disagreement, in the various market newsletters that are published.*

Looking ahead for the next few years, the most likely major depressant of the market is the gold stocks under U.S. control or

---

*See Appendix C for a partial listing.

influence. These are, first, the $12 billion in bullion (calculated at $35 per ounce), mostly in less than "good delivery" bars, in Fort Knox and elsewhere. And second, the IMF overhang of 25 million ounces, plus another 100 million ounces to be exchanged for paper securities.

These stocks give the U.S. an ability to create uncertainty in the market. But in point of fact, the United States seems notably unwilling to dispose of its gold reserve *in toto*. There are far more words than action — more noise, with propaganda, than deeds, by emptying the vaults — in the U.S. strategy. Moreover, the International Monetary Fund is subject to tight constraints, both from its European members who are unwilling to see their gold assets decline in value, and from the underdeveloped countries, who are looking for a "free lunch." In brief, the potential for uncertainty is great (and undoubtedly will be utilized by the United States to the utmost), but unless Washington loses its head completely, it will not sell off its gold stocks, nor even any large portion of it.

Over a short to medium-term outlook of several years, these depressants are counterbalanced by the incipient collapse of the debt pyramid and the oft-recurring currency crises around the world which usually (but not always) send weak currency holders scrambling for gold bullion. We also have random world events which trigger a spurt in gold sales, such as the death of Chou En-lai in January 1976, which reportedly promoted Far East buying in anticipation of a more hawkish Chinese approach to foreign policy.

What happens in the United States politically and economically is the starting point for any analysis of future gold markets. On the assumption that the U.S. persists in its "something-for-nothing" politicized economic policies, coupled with a war on gold to protect the paper factory output of fiat money, then it is reasonably easy to predict the broad outlines of the outcome. This Doomsday policy is generating larger and larger budgetary deficits. For the fiscal year ending June 30, 1975, the Federal deficit reached $64.60 billion. The following year the deficit was more than fifty percent larger. For the fiscal year ending June 30, 1976, it totalled an incredible $98.00 billion. These monumental deficits have to be monetized and are therefore inflationary, sooner or later.

CHART 10-3: FACTORS DETERMINING THE PRICE OF GOLD

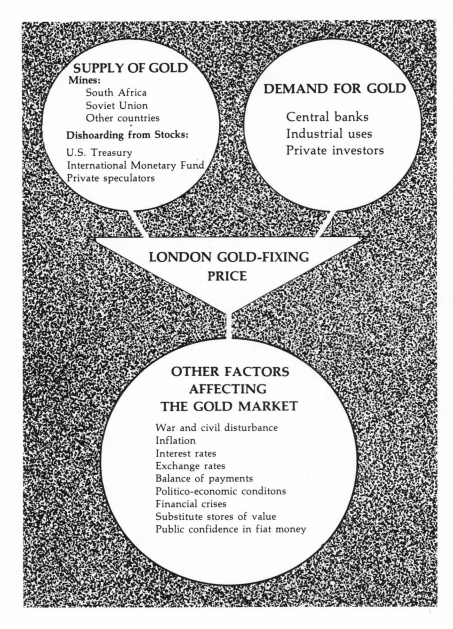

SUPPLY OF GOLD
Mines:
　　South Africa
　　Soviet Union
　　Other countries
Dishoarding from Stocks:
U.S. Treasury
International Monetary Fund
Private speculators

DEMAND FOR GOLD

Central banks
Industrial uses
Private investors

LONDON GOLD-FIXING
PRICE

OTHER FACTORS
AFFECTING
THE GOLD MARKET

War and civil disturbance
Inflation
Interest rates
Exchange rates
Balance of payments
Politico-economic conditons
Financial crises
Substitute stores of value
Public confidence in fiat money

On the assumption that politicians will continue to act like politicians, then our socialist economy will continue to generate inflation, partly to continue vote-buying policies but increasingly to maintain liquidity in the economy, as various sectors of the debt structure begin to collapse under the load of past debt and regulation-induced inefficiencies.

Inflation always leads to depression, so it can readily be seen that the inflation-depression cycles of the past decades will begin to acquire greater amplitude — but perhaps in disguised form as the cycles start to lag and overlap. The end of it all will be an inflationary collapse of the paper factory, with the possibility of a deflationary collapse in some sectors (such as real estate and municipal bonds) in the midst of general hyperinflation. (The English call what they have "slumpflation," so this would be "hyper-slumpflation.") Investment advisor Thomas J. Holt and others have long made such predictions. More recently, even Michael J. Evans, president of Chase Econometrics, predicted double-digit inflation in 1977 and the worst recession ever in 1978.*

Sophisticated investors are watching this linked sequence of events. Money supply figures are carefully monitored. The Federal Reserve Bank of St. Louis publishes weekly estimates of M_1, the money supply in the U.S., and M_2, the broader-based money supply aggregate. Many analysts believe these figures reveal inflationary trends six to twelve months in advance. More specifically, some money-supply watchers look for an increase in short-term interest rates, coupled with an increase in business loans, as the inflationary trigger. This anticipation of inflation is linked to anticipation of a run to gold as a protection against inflation. When the signs point to more inflation, gold purchases increase, and thus gold prices begin to move upwards. These can be temporarily dampened by Treasury auctions, but if either South Africa or Russia withholds its sales of newly mined gold, the price can take off like a rocket. In previous run-ups the private offtake has accounted for almost all trade. The European central banks have a vested interest in higher gold prices, to increase the value of their gold reserves, and thus improve

---

*Quoted in *Financial Mail*, Johannesburg, South Africa; October 31, 1975, p. 437.

their balance sheets. They will also be alert to see that the price of gold doesn't fall through the floor.

Gold mining shares normally move with gold, but lag behind the gold price and inflationary anticipations. However, the multiplier in gold mining shares is greater and the rate of increase in price is greater than that of gold itself. Thus we have a linked sequence: when money supply increases, it is a signal of further inflation to follow; these anticipations cause investors and speculators to turn toward gold, and then to gold-mining shares, as a protection against the ravages of inflation.

The diagram reproduced earlier, on page 79, shows why this has been a sound strategy in the past. And why this same sequence will undoubtedly be followed in the future — until gold is the acknowledged victor in the conflict now being waged.

CHAPTER ELEVEN

The Assault on South Africa

The interests and general welfare of the Transkei are so intimately interwoven with those of South Africa, that an attack on the one would mean aggression against the other. . . . Should it become necessary, the soldiers of the Transkei would fight shoulder to shoulder with the soldiers of South Africa.

Paramount Chief K. D. Matanzima, Chief Minister of the Transkei, on founding of the Transkei Army, (*Die Burger*, Cape Town, December 11, 1975, p. 2).

SOUTH AFRICA ALONE PRODUCES TWO-THIRDS of the world's newly mined gold and, not coincidentally, is the target of a furious worldwide attack for her policies of apartheid, or "separate development." The self-serving nature of these relentless attacks and the ambivalent role of the United States, which talks out of one side of its mouth on one day but the other side on the next, suggest we look more closely at South Africa's role in the war on gold.

What is the link between the worldwide attack on South Africa and her position as the number-one producer of gold? As the premier gold producer in the world, South Africa quite naturally has been a strong proponent of gold as the cornerstone of a rational monetary system. This is a self-interested policy, to be sure; but the arguments for gold are historically valid and stand quite apart from South Africa. Indeed, so far in this study we have scarcely mentioned the world's largest producer by name. South Africa has also produced some eloquent spokesmen for gold we can refer to in passing, but their logic and eloquence are not a central factor in the war on gold, which tends to revolve around Northern Hemisphere figures. The States President Dr. N. Diederichs, former Minister of Finance, known in South Africa as "Mr. Gold," has naturally made many caustic comments on paper money, among his pithy observations on life in general. For example:

> History has shown that Ministers of Finance have always been the ones who have been threatened with death. More have been tortured and hanged as a result of taxes they have imposed than generals have been as a result of losing wars. In France from 1315 to 1781, thirty-seven Ministers of Finance lost their lives through being tortured and hanged. You see what dangerous work we have. It is undoubtedly one of the riskiest professions in life.*

Neither Dr. Diederichs nor any other South African has publicly expounded the real reasons for the U.S. war on gold and the worldwide assault on South Africa. Diederichs suggests the hostile attitude of the United States has more to do with the U.S. balance-of-payments deficits than any fundamental ideological persuasion. Possibly the South Africans don't know of any more fundamental reasons. Possibly South Africans are too polite or too politic to point the accusing finger at the world's most powerful state. So let us first take a look at U.S. policy towards South Africa, then at the South African internal background, and finally at the origins of the contemporary war on gold.

South Africa and the United States

Acceptance of South Africa by the U.S. Establishment depends how far one probes below surface reporting. Meetings

---

Argus (Cape Town, South Africa), January 30, 1975.

between high-level officials reportedly are cordial. From time to time Treasury Secretary Simon or Secretary of State Kissinger issued public reassurances that the two countries maintain friendly relations, and their successors will probably do the same.

But just below this public affability is official coolness. When Secretary Kissinger visited Africa in April 1976, he pointedly avoided visiting South Africa, while issuing numerous press statements about the manner in which the South Africans should run their internal affairs. There is a strict U.S. arms embargo on South Africa. In the words of former Assistant Secretary of State David D. Newsom, "We have done so as a tangible demonstration of our support of self-determination and our desire to avoid any support for the imposition of apartheid."*

Compare this statement to the decades-long economic and military support of the Soviet Union by the U.S.,† 100,000 Americans killed in Korea and Vietnam with arms supplied by Russia, and the professed intent of *détente*: trade with the Soviet Union to bring about world peace (which in practice has the effect of subsidizing Soviet imperialism). Minority single-party rule by the Communist Party in the U.S.S.R. is quite acceptable to the U.S. Establishment, but not minority *multi*-party rule in South Africa. The concept of "self determination" can be ignored in the case of the U.S.S.R., but not apparently in the case of South Africa. Moreover, the "self-determination" concept that is explicitly built into the South African "homelands" policy is not even recognized by the United States. Products which are approved for shipment to the U.S.S.R. are banned for South Africa, such as oscilloscopes, automotive parts, aircraft communications systems, and aircraft engines.‡ In the words of Secretary Newson:

> *I know of no other country [than the U.S.] which makes as conscientious an effort to survey and to administer, if you will, the non-military exports with*

---

*House of Representatives, *Implementation of the U.S. Arms Embargo*, Hearings before the Subcommittee on Africa of the Committee on Foreign Affairs, (Washington: 1973).

†See Antony C. Sutton, *National Suicide: Military Aid to The Soviet Union*, (New York: Arlington House Publishers, 1973). Also see bibliography for related books.

‡*Ibid.*, p. 145-6.

military implications to these areas of Southern Africa. *

The pertinent question is, Why does the United States ban civilian goods to South Africa, but not to the Soviet Union? The Soviet Union has internal policies that are far more reprehensible and has been directly responsible for the deaths of 100,000 Americans. We might also ask why, if *détente* with the Soviet Union will bring peace, as Republican and Democratic officials have repeatedly asserted, then would not *détente* with South Africa also be beneficial? The answers to these questions bear directly on the war on gold.

First, we should take a closer look at the South African problem. South Africans have embarked on a unique experiment. And in the light of the turmoil in South Boston and other urban American conflicts, it is an experiment the United States would do well to observe, rather than reject out of hand. Given the choice of sharing political power between black and white in a single political unit or dividing South Africa into independent black and white states, each to live according to its own cultural traditions and mores, South Africa has chosen the latter road. For instance the Transkei, an independently sovereign black state, received full independence in October 1976. This policy in some ways approximates the Black Muslim proposals for the United States, that black and white cultures should be allowed to develop separately, according to their own mores and objectives.

It is a policy that has not gone unnoticed among honest blacks in the United States. For example, former Black Panther leader Eldridge Cleaver, who unlike most critics of South Africa has himself lived in Africa, has stated: ". . . blacks in white-ruled South Africa and Rhodesia have more freedom than blacks in dictatorial Uganda." Cleaver accused American blacks of "playing a political game based on skin color," and said that the struggle in Africa is not one of color but of ruthless oppression by dictatorial states (among which he does *not* include South Africa and Rhodesia). By contrast, Marxist Cuba is cited as a country where "officials are white and the masses black." Says Cleaver, "I took this up with the Cuban Communist Party. They told me the

---

Ibid., p. 151.

things they used to tell us in the 1930s. 'Well they ain't ready yet. Not enough of them are educated.' ''*

In addition, there are major internal changes underway in Southern Africa. These fall into two areas:

(a) *détente* with Black Africa, at the initiative of South African Prime Minister Vorster, involving Zambia, Ivory Coast, Tanzania, and Mozambique; and,

(b) internal changes eliminating "petty apartheid" and absorbing the "coloreds" into the political structure.

These changes have to be seen against a background little understood outside South Africa. South Africa is an extraordinarily complex society. It has distinct European cultures, predominantly Afrikaner and English; it has Asian cultures, predominantly Indian, with their own religions and cultures; and it has nine distinct Bantu races with their own languages. One practical problem that strikes any observant visitor is that for a black to work efficiently in Pretoria, for instance, he has to be trilingual. South Africa is aware that such ethnic differences and contacts have led to conflict elsewhere. The country intends to avoid the problems of north-versus-south that have divided nations; the racial conflicts that have occurred in Boston, Watts, and scores of other American cities; the Kurdish revolts; and a thousand similar episodes in history. Who is to say they are wrong? An "expert" sociologist living 10,000 miles away, who has been no nearer South Africa than Long Island?

Objectivity suggests we should at least admit that nothing else has solved these problems, and give the South African approach a chance. Yet in October 1975, an Assistant Secretary of State falsely accused South Africa of imprisoning critics of apartheid. This accusation was flatly rejected as untrue and the official was asked by South Africa what evidence he had to support his accusation. None was forthcoming. The State Department *had* no evidence; the story was a lie.

What have these episodes to do with the war on gold?

As we probe deeper, we find that hostility to South Africa has gone so far that plans for military attack on the nation have been drafted. Such contingency plans do much to explain the

---

*Associated Press, May 17, 1976.

strict arms embargo against South Africa as well as the persistent, labored, and often false attacks on "separate development" and the South African approach to its internal affairs.
These invasion plans, along with the war on gold itself, originate
at the core of the Wall Street liberal Establishment, which domin-
ates U.S. foreign and domestic policy. It is at this "behind-the-
scenes" decision-making level that we discover what appears to
be the ultimate intention of the United States. It is at this level
that demands for a war on gold began, surfacing as far back as
1965 and specifically designed to break South Africa's financial
back — perhaps as a prelude to military invasion. (The armchair
generals in New York underestimated the resiliency of the South
African economy, however. The 1975 devaluation, a tough 1976
budget, and a gold-currency swap stabilized the economy.)

So the basic reason for the attack on South Africa has little to
do with its racial or domestic policies; these are propaganda
counterparts to the war on gold. A moment's thought will suggest that a Kissinger who is unmoved by Soviet persecution of
Jews and political dissidents is unlikely to be moved by the lack of
voting rights for black South Africans. The basic reason for the
anti-South African hostility is that South Africa is a geological
freak, a vast storehouse of mineral wealth, and an inviting target
for every imperialist cabal in the world — the Soviet Union and
the United States included.

The Carnegie Endowment and the War on Gold

In 1965 the tax-exempt Carnegie Endowment for International Peace, ostensibly studying ways to end black persecution in South Africa, published a study detailing how a United
Nations attack could be made on South Africa.* The report
quoted military calculations including the number of troops required for the attack (93,000), the air power required (3,000 fly-
ing hours), and the estimated casualties expected (18,900 to
37,800, with the added comment that "a percentage of these
personnel would be returned to duty").

We can put to one side the obviously gross underestimates
by the presumably amateur generals at the Carnegie Endowment.

---

*Amelie C. Leiss, *Apartheid and United Nations Collective Measures*, (New York:
Carnegie Endowment for International Peace, 1965).

More pertinently, how does a tax-exempt "peace" foundation get tangled up in promoting wars on the world's largest producer of gold?

The 1965 Carnegie Report, with its shrill accusations recommending aggression against South Africa, was signed by Joseph E. Johnson, president of the foundation. Johnson is less well-known for another position he holds: Honorary Secretary General (for the United States) for the Bilderberger meetings. Prince Bernhard of the Netherlands (of Lockheed payoff fame) is chairman of the Bilderberger group. The Bilderberger group, supposedly dedicated to strengthening Western ideals, is in practice in the forefront of creating a collectivist one-world new order. Such a New World Order would of course be under U.S. (that is, Wall Street) dominance. In other words, it would be the same dollar imperialism that is at the root of the war on gold.

In brief, the Carnegie Endowment is an integral part of the U.S. Establishment; in many ways it is closer to the center of policy making than the Washington bureaucrats. The Carnegie Endowment has a vested interest in promoting dollar imperialism. Why not a "collective attack" on the Soviet Union, where Jews and political dissidents are more persecuted than any black laborer in South Africa? Why was no voice raised by the Endowment against South Africa in World War II or Korea, when "petty apartheid" was more rigid than today? Why is there no recognition of the significant changes that have occurred in South Africa?

As part of the Carnegie program to "alter the future" on behalf of dollar imperialism, the Leiss Report of the foundation recommended a boycott on gold as a prelude to military action. This 1965 report noted that export of gold and gold by-products accounts for 77 percent of the gross national product. Gold is "the most important single earner of foreign exchange," the Carnegie report stressed. The "study" also introduced some shaky reasoning to contend that gold mining would decline before 1970 and predicted that, "by 1981, only four of the existing mines on the Witaterstrand may still be in production."*

The Leiss Report concluded that, "it would be next to impossible to prevent gold from moving into trade channels even if

---

*Leiss Report, *op. cit.*, p. 114.

complete economic measures were applied." It observed that, "a successful boycott on gold would, if followed, either require some extremely intensive policing operations or some method of shutting off the market or a part of it."* In other words, merely calling for a boycott would not be sufficient; force would be required to make it stick.

Getting such a program implemented would create problems for the United States, of course. So the report raised the question, "Which would be more damaged by a successful boycott on South African gold, South Africa or the system of international liquidity?"

The report then offered the obvious conclusion: the only way by which the benefits of South African gold could be denied to South Africa, without destroying international trade, is to destroy the *price* of gold — while at the same time maintaining U.S. gold reserves to preserve U.S. liquidity and to make the reserves available for strategic purposes.

In practice, the Carnegie Endowment proposal has been the policy adopted by the United States. Psychological warfare has been mounted against gold and against South Africa, the largest producer of gold. While promoting a war on gold, however, the United States has been careful to maintain its own gold reserves.

In 1975 the Russian-Cuban takeover of Angola provided a spine-chilling confirmation that the "Carnegie Plan" for military action against South Africa is entering its final phase. In the past two years the attack on the price of gold by the U.S. Treasury and the U.S.-dominated International Monetary Fund has been a major factor in keeping the price level of gold as low as $120 to $140 an ounce. Publicly, the U.S. position on the takeover of Angola was an uncomfortable "hands-off." But in fact the U.S. was working at the time against South Africa, and the Marxist conquest of Angola fitted into that plan. Secretary of State Henry Kissinger personally reassured leaders of Latin America's Marxist governments that the U.S. would remain on the sidelines of the conflict in Angola, although some public announcements would be made criticizing the Russian-Cuba takeover. The statements would be designed to appease the American public, however, not

---

Ibid., p. 121.

upset the plans for Angola. Reports Washington columnist Paul Scott:

> . . . *the Kissinger warning is taken by insiders as an old diplomatic trick used by a government that wants to appear like it is taking a strong stand, while in effect doing nothing about a serious threat.* *

In Peru, Kissinger assured President Morales Bermudez, Castro's close friend, that the U.S. had no real intention of supporting South Africa's action against the Cubans in Angola. Later, when the Senate Foreign Relations Committee questioned Kissinger about a Presidential request for aid to the FNLA-China-South African alliance fighting the Russian-Cuban-MPLA side, Kissinger replied: "The request was only a diplomatic gesture."

The *London Economist* quoted intelligence sources to the effect that the United States played a double game in Angola: the CIA promised South Africa military support against the Marxist MPLA — and then reneged on its pledge. In brief, the report suggests, the United States led South Africa into a trap.

This may sound incredible to many readers, but note that this interpretation and the facts are both consistent with three basic realities: the war on gold, the propaganda war against South Africa, and the arms embargo on South Africa. Further, they are consistent with the 50-year-old alliance between the capitalist autocracy on Wall Street and the Bolshevik autocracy in Moscow.†

In sum, Wall Street is quite happy to see Angola as a Marxist colony. Gulf Oil, which is dominated by the Mellon interests, could hardly wait to turn over oil production royalties to the Marxists and get the Gulf oil fields back into production. The State Department, of all institutions, had to restrain Gulf Oil. So much for our "anti-communist" capitalists.

---

*"Kissinger's cover operation," *Utah Independent*, March 4, 1976.

†See Antony C. Sutton, *Wall Street and the Bolshevik Revolution*, (New York: Arlington House Publishers, 1974), which presents evidence of a Wall Street (Morgan-Rockefeller) collusion with the Bolsheviks to overthrow the Constitutional government of Russia in 1917. Henry Kissinger is a long-time Rockefeller protegé from the same Wall Street Establishment that contains Gulf Oil (Mellon), with its royalty donations to the Angola Marxists, and the Carnegie Endowment, with its military planning studies for aggression against South Africa.

But is Wall Street also prepared to see South Africa become a Soviet colony, with South African gold added to Soviet production? We will take a look at that interesting question in the next chapter.

In light of the above, it can be argued that the attack on South African racial policies is nothing more than a cover for a politico-military attack on South Africa, for which the war on gold is an essential preliminary, and in which gold and mineral wealth are the ultimate objectives.

The war on South African gold originated with the Wall Street Establishment. But this is not the place to more than hint at the complete story of Wall Street's incredible machinations. The interested reader is referred to the Wall Street involvement in the 1917 Bolshevik Revolution, the continuing military and economic assistance to and protection of the Soviet Union by the Wall Street banking establishment,* and the drive for a New World Order under U.S. dominance (which means dollar imperialism under Wall Street leadership), in which the U.S.S.R. would become a technical and financial colony of the United States.

The war on gold is a major part of the *external* aspect of this imperialistic drive. It also supports the *internal* thrust for a controlled and manipulated U.S. economy, through the paper factory of the Federal Reserve System.† The 1965 study by the Carnegie Endowment for International Peace, the Leiss Report, was no accident. It was a trial balloon proposing a military invasion of a friendly nation; the report emphasized the "necessity" for a preliminary cold war on gold to break the financial back of South Africa.

In the epigraph to this chapter, we quoted a black South African responding to outside threats. That whites, both Afrikaner and English, will fiercely defend South Africa against *any* attack (whether sponsored by the United States, the Soviet Union, the United Nations, or a combination of all three) is obvious to anyone who knows the country and its people. That blacks will also defend the beleagured nation on Africa's crucial

---

*This aspect will be explored more fully in the author's next book, *The Paper Factory*, which should be released in the spring of 1978.

†See Appendix B.

tip will surprise many of the armchair revolutionaries in Washington and New York.

CHAPTER TWELVE

Gold Is Dead, Isn't It?

Those who do not accept gold as the basis of the world's currency system may still be persuaded that it should be retained as an alternative. If the present attempt to run the world system on floating paper currencies fails, and I can see no reason to expect it to succeed, then the gold alternative will be needed. At the moment, it is vitally important that the gold alternative should be preserved, even if it cannot yet be restored.

William Rees-Mogg, Editor, *The Times* (London).

HISTORICALLY, WARS ON GOLD HAVE BEEN ASSOCIATED with tyranny and totalitarian grabs for political power. When gold coins circulate freely alongside paper money (as occurred with the Continental bill and the Greenback in the United States, and the British paper pound of 1797), gold will be valued more than paper money. Following the inexorable law of the market place, the paper currency will be placed at a discount. But when a political power base is threatened by these superior competitive characteristics of gold, too often the paper currency or debt is declared as the *only* legal money, to the exclusion of gold (*e.g.*, the cases of Kubla Khan, John Law's Banque Royale, and the Federal Reserve dollar). Sooner or later in the war on gold, physical coercion has to be used to impose such a politicized fiat money on an unwilling citizenry.

Our contermporary war on gold began internally with the establishment of the Federal Reserve System in 1913 and externally with the Genoa Conference of 1922, which introduced the gold *exchange* standard. Coercive aspects were introduced internally in 1934, when President Franklin D. Roosevelt confiscated American gold. The coercive character was confirmed internationally in 1971, when President Richard M. Nixon suspended convertibility of the dollar into gold. The legalization of gold in the United States in 1975 was probably not a withdrawal from coercion but an interim effort to make the propaganda war on gold more credible. History suggests that gold will once again be made illegal in the United States and subject to arbitrary seizure by a police-state apparatus.

Looking back over monetary history, we see that gold has *always* been prominent as a protector of individual sovereignty. Private gold ownership is inconsistent with the aims of dictatorship; a war on gold is a necessary concomitant to centralized political power. Wars and fiat currencies have always gone hand in hand. From the 800-year-old Byzantine Empire, which traded from one end of the known world to the other, to the industrialization of nineteenth-century Europe and the United States, we see that economic prosperity was based on gold-stabilized monetary systems. Significantly, throughout history those eras of gold-backed currency stability became platforms for sustained economic advances.

Those were eras of relative peace and prosperity. France was on the gold standard for 100 years, from 1814 to 1914; Switzerland for 86 years, from 1850 to 1936. Other European countries based their industrial progress on the monetary stability of the gold standard. Far from being restrictive and denying liquidity, as our modern internationalists have claimed, the gold standard is a stable framework within which a free civilization can advance, perhaps not with spectacular "something-for-everyone" welfare programs but certainly with solid, respectable growth that does not collapse into inflationary-deflationary spirals (or "slumpflation," as they describe it in England).

What then is the rationale behind the contemporary war on gold?

In the final analysis the current — and continuing — war on gold is a political power play of almost incredible proportions. To ignore the political aims of the paper fanatics, by looking only at the monetary aspects, is to ignore the full breadth and scope of the modern drive towards what has been called a New World Order. The discipline of gold has always restricted political schemers, whether they be John Law, John Maynard Keynes, or today's Wall Street internationalists. Money is power. Gold is a universal and timeless money, unexcelled as a store of value, usually available only to those who will yield scarce resources to gain it. Paper money and debt money, by contrast, can be easily created. With a fiat paper-money currency, power can be created by whomever has the legal monopoly of the creation process. Who owns the paper factory controls the system. Paper money or debt creation is flexible, infinitely expandable, ersatz money. It is precisely this ersatz quality of paper and debt money that makes it politically useful and desirable to the power brokers. It can be manipulated. Gold cannot be manipulated politically, therefore it is unusable and undesirable.

When the supply of this ersatz money is inflated (by an increase of bank credit, printing bank notes, or creating IMF Special Drawing Rights), one does not *pari passu* increase the amount of goods and services available. The result therefore is price inflation: More money is available to purchase the same amount of goods; as the artificial fiat money works its way into the economic system, more paper claims are demanded per unit of goods. This bidding up of prices is unavoidable and has always led to depreciation of paper money. The inevitable end of the road occurs when the paper has zero value: the German 1923 and 1946 mark, the Hungarian pengo, the Greek drachma are just a few of several hundred examples where countries left the gold standard, embarked on a paper money excursion, and saw their economy crash as their currencies ended up worthless.

Of course, gold can, and has, led to price inflation. But gold is limited in supply by natural factors and requires scarce resources to produce. Therefore it has nowhere near the same ability to generate price increases as do paper-debt systems.

Today a gigantic, multi-trillion dollar* pyramid of illiquid, paper debt is poised precariously on a small tip of liquid, tangible gold. Everybody's paper fiat money and credit line is someone else's debt. And the U.S. Treasury, so it claims, is going to dispose of the liquid gold tip of the pyramid!

In any war on gold, two factors always emerge to entice holders of paper money and illiquid debt to substitute gold (or other tangible assets) for their fantasy fiat holdings. Price increases encourage a search for a reliable store of wealth. Traditionally, gold has been the store of wealth of last resort. Then, institutional failures encourage a search for safe investments, as the owners and paper wealth become more concerned with the security of liquid assets than producing more paper profits. Gold produces no income, it is a sterile way to hold wealth, but it protects both liquidity and value in storage.

During the last few years in the contemporary war on gold, there have been price upswings touching 35-percent per annum in Europe and ten percent in the United States. The depression of 1974-1975 generated cracks in the illiquid debt structure — most obviously in the real estate and banking sectors. In the years ahead, subsequent boom-and-depression cycles will have even greater amplitude, with double-digit price increases (including double-digit interest rates), followed by the complete collapse of some sectors of the debt pyramid.†

For individuals, hyperinflation and the collapse of some sectors will breed a *sauve qui peut* attitude; there will be a mad scramble for gold and other tangible wealth. Holders of paper money will follow Tom Paine's injunction of two hundred years ago:

The question for the people to ask, and the only question, is this: whether the quantity of Bank Notes,

---

*There are different ways to calculate the debt pyramid. The National Taxpayers Union estimates that there is $5 *trillion* in government debt alone today.

†Europe operates on different cycles than the United States. For example, secondary banking collapsed in the United Kingdom in the last few years, while in the U.S. banking has only reached the "problem list" stage.

*payable on demand, which the Bank has issued, be
greater than the Bank can pay off in Gold and Silver.* *

As we look into the future (in competition with the professional prognosticators), the domestic war on gold looks like this:
there will be an increasing realization by the public that the ratio
between paper-debt and gold is inexorably shifting in favor of
gold. That public confidence is the all-important requirement to
keep a paper-debt money system afloat . . . and this confidence
is eroding. Surges in confidence-erosion will account for short-
run increases in the price of gold, while for intermittent periods
the government will regain some public confidence; when this
occurs, gold will settle back to its approximate long-run ratio to
paper-debt units.

At some point, however, there is a distinct probability of
panic — *if* debt holders see the debt pyramid collapsing or even
anticipate its collapse. Particularly this will be true if there is a
general realization that paper assets are actually someone else's
debt and are inherently worthless. However, it is important to
note a distinction between "realization" and "action." Investors
may "know" the pyramid is illiquid and in danger of collapse;
they may not "act" on this knowledge. The herd instinct suggests that only a few will bale out in time; the majority will act
in panic, too late.

Any panic-induced scramble for tangible assets (of which
gold is the historical leader) could eat up the IMF's 100-million
ounces of gold and all of the Fort Knox reserves *in a few weeks,
if not days*. It is highly significant that in the gold pool scramble,
the private offtake of gold equalled 2,500 tons in two years —
and in the 1967 dash for gold, the average investor was not even
in the race. The upside potential for gold prices in a panic environment is awe-inspiring. Precisely because of the gigantic size of
the debt pyramid, any figures become meaningless: how many
assignats, or 1923 German marks, or Hungarian pengos does it
take *today* to buy one ounce of gold?

A downside support to the price of gold stems from the
unwillingness of European central banks to see their reserve

---

*Quoted in Cobbett, *op. cit.*, p. 141.

assets decline in value, even in the short run. There is an increasing realization by the investing public and institutions that central banks do indeed have a stake in gold.

The basics of the problem must always be held in mind, and the basics derive from a distillation of historical experience, not the self-promoting meanderings of contemporary academic economists or the power objectives of the New World Order imperialists.

The basic question we should hold in mind is: What is money? The answer to that is: Money is whatever people think it is. Money is a commodity that people agree, mutually and voluntarily, to use in exchange for goods and services, one that possesses a store of value. Money must be credible and believable. If its worth is a fiction, it must be a *credible* fiction. A government may decree what can be used as legal tender; it cannot arbitrarily decree what will be accepted as money. There are dozens of historical examples that confirm the basic lesson: People in the process of exchange with each other use as money that which they prefer, that commodity which best fulfills the need for money, not that which a government dictates, however harsh the edict may be.

How do the basic specifications for a desirable money conform with the use of SDRs, fiat Federal Reserve notes, and debt money in general? They do not. Special Drawing Rights (SDRs) are not even paper money, they are computer entries — electrical impulses fed to the IMF computer in Washington, D.C. SDRs can be expanded or contracted by the actions of a computer operator; they are subject both to random and to arbitrary action. In January 1975, for example, the IMF increased members' borrowing rights by 40 percent after ten minutes of discussion. But such "borrowing rights" have no valid claim on real tangible assets.

The *declared* intent for these new reserve assets and paper-debt systems is to reduce the monetary role of gold in the international order. The fallacy is that this claim ignores the truism that arbitrary decrees cannot dictate what is used as money. Demonetization of the dollar, by suspending convertibility, does not suspend the use of gold; nor does it change the intrinsic qualities of gold. Moreover, gold purchases in the market place by the European central banks suggest that the demonetization of gold has not been accepted outside the United States and England. After the 1976 IMF Jamaica Conference, French Finance Minister Fourade announced that France would buy IMF gold in order to "harmonize the composition of its gold and currency reserves." Fritz Leutwiler, president of the Swiss National Bank, has indicated skepticism about the wisdom and the practicality of expelling gold from the world monetary scene. Leutwiler said, "Switzerland is not keen on joining this ideological crusade."

The basic value of gold therefore remains — along with constant reminders that gold will be very much acceptable as money when the paper stuff has lost credibility. In 1974 Italy floated a loan from West Germany, backed by gold collateral valued at $120 an ounce. In February 1976 Portugal borrowed $250 million from German central banks, backed with gold as collateral; another loan of $50 million from Switzerland was also backed by gold. But note that Italy and Portugal had no alternative. No country or banker will, at the moment, accept Italian paper lire or Portugal's paper escudos as collateral for a loan. Gold has been and will remain a more than adequate security.

In May 1976 the Great Western United Corporation introduced a gold-silver payment clause in its sugar purchase agreement with Azucarera la Victoria de Panama. It did so to protect itself against inflation in Panama; it did not want future claims to be paid in worthless paper currencies. This contract required a Great Western subsidiary to raise $150 million for the purchase of gold and silver bullion to place in inventory.*

The foregoing discussion does not explain *why* the United States decided to declare war on gold. Perhaps the U.S. now has no alternative, given the impending collapse of its debt structure. Be that as it may, the essential reason more probably is that as far back as 1913 (and maybe before), the Wall Street Establishment had well-defined ideas about the kind of world it wanted to achieve with its financial power. The pattern for a New World Order, the Rockefeller-Wall Street plan for international power fueled by dollar imperialism, is now taking

---

Wall Street Journal, June 3, 1976. If such contracts become widespread, and substantial bullion inventories become commonplace in the business world, then the demand for gold and silver will increase astronomically.

shape. The Soviet Union has been reduced to the role of a technical captive. No doubt it is restive at times, but Henry Kissinger to the contrary, it is ultimately dependent on the West for technology. At the moment, Wall Street permits the Soviet Union to expand its influence around the world, no doubt because Marxist states provide the Wall Street internationalists with lucrative, non-competitive markets. A dependent dictatorship is a safe customer.

After South Africa, Western Europe is next in line to succumb to Marxist totalitarian rule. If this occurs, it would place most of the world in technical and financial subservience to the Wall Street Establishment, because every new Marxist state is a guaranteed customer for American technology.

Gold has a key role in the construction of this New World Order. Dollar imperialism requires supremacy of the dollar. But the dollar is inconvertible paper; it can be challenged by gold — *and only by gold*. The major producers of gold are:

(a) the Soviet Union, which at the moment presents no real threat to the United States because of its technical dependence; and

(b) South Africa, which *is* a threat, because receipts of its gold sales are only slightly influenced by Wall Street's ambitions.

South Africa is becoming increasingly independent of the United States. It is doing so deliberately, as a matter of survival. By contrast, the Soviet Union, with its perennial crop failures and its continuing heavy technological requirements, is becoming more dependent on the West, particularly the United States.

Consequently, South Africa is an unwitting barrier to the New World Order. When Mozambique was seized by Marxists the United States did nothing to hinder the change of power (although it was careful to preserve its anti-Marxist public image). When Angola fell to Marxists, the United States again made a *pretence* of support and sympathy for the non-Marxist side . . . but that was all.

We know from historical experience that economic and financial conflict can be a prelude to physical conflict. Even without subscribing to the Marxist economic theory of class war and dollar imperialism, we can cite the Mafeking Raid and the Anglo-Boer war in South Africa, both of which were heavily influenced by the gold and diamond discoveries of the late nineteenth century.

Could the war on gold then escalate into a U.S. attack on South Africa, to control an independent gold source and an irritable challenge to the New World Order? Or alternatively (and more easily disguised from the American public), might the United States encourage the Soviet Union to move against South Africa? From the evidence presented in Chapter Eleven, it seems Henry Kissinger and his friends have been doing precisely that. From the Establishment viewpoint, a gold supply even under Soviet influence would be preferred to one controlled by an independent South Africa.

The Soviet Union is dependent on the U.S. for wheat and advanced technology and uses gold to pay for these supplies. South Africa is not dependent on the United States for anything. Consequently, ownership of South African gold would enable the Soviet Union to become an even greater market for Western technology. In brief, the United States could eliminate its troublesome gold problem *and* gain a rich new captive market overnight! (Or within the 130 days which the Carnegie Endowment for International Peace estimates it would require to occupy South Africa.)

This may sound fantastic reasoning — but perhaps not so fantastic to readers outside the United States. There are signs even now of the implementation of such policy.* As we noted in Chapter Eleven, in 1965 the tax-exempt Carnegie Endowment for International Peace issued a report categorizing the military forces needed for an attack on South Africa by "France, West Germany, the Soviet Union, the United Kingdom and the United States."†

If this indeed is the hidden policy of the United States, then one critical observation appears to have escaped our Establishment planners (that is, presuming that they are not intentionally planning our — and their — destruction). Every major

---

*The reader is referred to the writer's *Wall Street and the Bolshevik Revolution, op. cit.,* for details of critical Wall Street assistance to the Bolsheviks, the first Marxist state. Covert U.S. support for a Soviet move against South Africa would be consistent with long-run U.S. policy *in practice.*

†*Ibid.,* p. 151.

civilization in history has been based on control of most of the available gold supply. We briefly described a few illustrations of this fact of history in Chapter One. Then there was the sixteenth-century Spanish empire, based on control of most of the world's then-known gold mines. The British Empire was at its most powerful when it controlled the world's gold mines in South Africa, Canada, and Australia. In recent decades, the United States has controlled the world's largest stockpile of gold, with reserves equal to twelve years of South African output.

Now look into the future. Soviet planners are not naive Keynesians or bemused *détenters*. They are blunt, ruthless realists. They recognize the simple equation: South African gold + Russian gold = nearly total world supply = world control.

Wall Street may think the U.S.S.R. is a safe technical captive of dollar imperialism. But it may be Wall Street and the rest of the non-Communist, half-heartedly free enterprise world that ends up as a captive of Russian imperialism. On this vital point the U.S. may have miscalculated.

In the past, any academic who dared to stress the implications of technical subsidy of the U.S.S.R. and our illogical gold policy has been scorned and harassed. Why? Because the Establishment does not have the skills to plan and analyze. It hires these skills. Mostly those they hire are self-promoting academics who suppress any evidence that is contrary to their brief. Those academics who stick to their last, which is teaching and research, are not going to be found near the power centers on a permanent basis. Occasionally, perhaps, they will be temporary and reluctant advisers. But it is the Kissingers, the Rostows, the Rusks, *et al*, who are found at the power centers. The advice they give suffers from the same deficiencies as their personal makeup. They are not well-founded in empirical knowledge. They lack a certain toughness of fiber. They tend to advise what is wanted, or what the Establishment client wants to hear. So their recommendations, based on faulty premises and ignorance and implemented hesitantly and half-heartedly, often fail. Have these academic sycophants misread the most logical result of their policies? We cannot say with certainty — and we hope that we will not learn the truth *ex post facto*.

In the final analysis, the international war on gold is a war for the gold output of South Africa, the world's largest producer. Apparently the United States is quite willing to see South Africa led, blindfolded, to the wall. Why? In part, at least, because the Keynesian bright boys in Washington have no concept of gold as a store of value — as *money* — and in foreign policy the Kissingerite bright boys are neither as tough nor as shrewd as the Soviet planners. Perhaps the Establishment believes it can control the Soviets by using U.S. technology as a carrot; or, Heaven forbid, as a stick — with American technical supremacy used as the world's peacemaker. There is no way the U.S. can control the U.S.S.R. merely through transfers of technology, for reasons too complex to analyze here.*

We have then reached our final conclusion, the distillation of our discussion: *The fate of South Africa, the world's largest gold producer, is also the fate of the United States.*

This conclusion may be repugnant to many persons whose assessments of South Africa are made from a distance of 10,000 miles, and whose closest proximity to a gold mine has been the United Nations Plaza in New York City. Let the reader be assured, however, that if South African gold falls (or is pushed) into Marxist hands, either directly or indirectly, then at some point down the road there will be no more Wall Street Establishment and no more United States as a free society. This will be the inexorable and inevitable consequence of the war on gold.

If our Establishment puts its fate, and ours, in the hands of anti-gold academicians and political planners, then they, and we, will pay the price. In warring on gold, the United States is flirting with a Doomsday demise of all American dreams. By tacitly subsidizing the Soviet mission in Africa, which is almost certainly aimed at South Africa's mineral wealth, the United States is writing *finis* to its own promises for human liberty; and it is condemning the world to a Soviet imperialism that allows no dissent and no objections.

It is not too late to call off a war in which the United States will be an even greater loser than South Africa. There is still time to restore integrity to our monetary policies and sanity to

---

*This author has written more on the topic of technical transfers to the U.S.S.R. than anyone else. If acreage in print is the test, he is more knowledgeable than anyone in Washington or New York about what can or cannot be accomplished to *control* the Soviets through economic assistance.

our foreign policies. But there is not much time. And once the pages of history are turned past our own point of no return, there is no second chance, no appeal to a higher court. It is now . . . or never.

APPENDIX A

LETTER SENT BY HUGHES, HUBBARD & REED (ATTORNEYS FOR NATIONAL COMMITTEE FOR MONETARY REFORM) TO SECRETARY OF THE TREASURY WILLIAM E. SIMON, JUNE 27, 1975.

Hughes Hubbard & Reed
1660 L Street, N.W.
Washington, D. C. 20036

June 27, 1975

BY HAND

The Honorable William E. Simon
Secretary of the Treasury
Department of the Treasury
15th Street & Pennsylvania Avenue
Washington, D.C. 20220

Dear Mr. Secretary:

I am writing on behalf of our client, the National Committee for Monetary Reform, and other interested persons, to object to the proposed sale of 500,000 ounces of gold on June 30, 1975, and to urge that you reject all bids submitted in connection with that proposed sale. There are several grounds for this objection.

First, despite the clear terms of the applicable provision of the Federal Property and Administrative Services Act of 1949, 40 U.S.C. § 484 (e) (2) (C), the proposed sale is scheduled to take place under the so-called "Dutch auction" method by which all bidders above the minimum acceptable bid will only have to pay the minimum amount for their purchases. This provision violates the Act by failing to secure the "most advantageous" price for the Government.

Second, despite the provisions of 40 U.S.C. § 484 (a) and (c) that the Administrator of General Services has the final authority to determine the proper conditions of the sale of "surplus government property," it is our understanding that these terms were set by the Treasury Department and not subject to the independent discretion of the Administrator of General Services.

Third, although the Federal Property and Administrative Services Act gives to the Administrator of General Services the statutory responsibility for deciding whether government property is truly "surplus" and therefore may lawfully be sold, 40 U.S.C. § 472 (g) and 484 (a), it is our understanding that the decision to sell gold as allegedly "surplus property" was made by the Treasury Department and was not subject to the independent discretion and decision of the Administrator of General Services.

Fourth, the determination to sell gold, particularly in bars of 250 troy ounces of .995 fineness, is evidently intended to depress the market price for gold. Bars of that size are not acceptable for delivery in international gold exchange. In addition, gold of at least .9995 fineness is necessary for "good delivery" in monetary transactions or for artistic uses. The demand for gold in such form is less intense than for "good delivery" gold. Before gold of such impurity could be used by purchasers, they would have to incur significant expenses in refining it. The choice of the weight and fineness of the gold to be sold will necessarily restrict demand and therefore will artificially depress the price which the Government will receive. Moreover, the exclusion of foreign governments and central banks (while nevertheless allowing foreign individuals and institutions to bid) will also artificially depress demand and thus reduce the market price for the gold. This proposed sale under circumstances calculated to obtain a depressed price for the property sold is inimical to the financial interests of the United States Government and the public, on whose behalf the Government owns the gold.

Fifth, the Treasury Department's policy of forcing down the price of gold, which is manifestly the objective of the scheduled sale on June 30th, is arbitrary, capricious, and unreasonable. The United States currently holds gold reserves of approximately 276 million ounces. The consequence of the Treasury Department's announced policy of depressing the price of gold has already caused a drop of at least $5 per ounce in the previously prevailing free market price. As a result, the value of the property of the United States (gold reserves) has been deliberately eroded by approximately $1.38 billion. Such a course violates the requirement of 31 U.S.C. § 733 that, when the Secretary of the Treasury sells gold, he must do so on terms "most advantageous to the public interest."

Sixth, under 31 U.S.C. § 354, the Bureau of the Mint must make an annual settlement of accounts of gold reserves. Under this obligation, the Treasury Department is required to take an annual physical inventory of gold bullion assets. In a letter to a Member of Congress dated September 5, 1974, the Secretary of the Treasury states that, under this provision, the Director of the Mint appoints annual settlement committees to take a physical inventory of assets at mints, assay offices, and bullion depositories. Nevertheless, the Comptroller General of the

United States in a report to Congress dated February 10, 1975 (B-87620) found that the last inventory of the Treasury's gold reserves was taken in 1953. It is arbitrary, capricious and unreasonable to sell significant quantities of gold, whether as "surplus property" or otherwise, without having made an audit or inventory according to generally accepted principles of inventory accounting to ascertain the amount and fineness of the Government's gold reserves.

We therefore urge you to reject all bids received in connection with the proposed June 30th sale and to desist from any further public sales of gold reserves that do not comply with the requirements of law.

Sincerely,

s/Philip A. Lacovara

APPENDIX B

BRIEFING BY THE AUTHOR ON INTERNATIONAL PROBLEMS FACING THE WEST, LONDON, ENGLAND, APRIL 1975.

Since 1958 this author has been interested in *how* the Soviet Union acquired its technology. Not *how much* technology the Soviets have, but *what kind* of technology and its origins. In other words, how Soviet innovation came about in practice, not in theory or propaganda.

By the early 1960s a working hypothesis emerged from the preliminary evidence. This hypothesis can now be supported with technical evidence from 1917 down to the present time. The hypothesis is that most Soviet technology has originated in Western enterprise countries. A rough estimate is that about 90 percent of Soviet technology has a Western origin. There is, of course, some indigenous Soviet technology, and in recent years there has even been a well-advertised flow of Soviet technology westwards. But these flows are relatively unimportant except for their propaganda value.

In brief, one cannot argue that *all* Soviet technology is of Western origin, but one can argue that the greater part of it is.

The reader will recall that the early 1960s was the era of Sputnik. Almost everybody was convinced that *of course* the Soviets were ahead of the United States in technology. Public opinion polls in England reported that most people thought the Soviets ahead of the United States in technology. In 1963 the writer gave a speech in Los Angeles, and a questioner asked "Who will get to the moon first, Russia or the United States?" The answer was that the Soviets could not get to the moon without United States help and technical assistance. The audience laughed. That was a huge joke!

So the early years of this research were slow going without assistance, but by 1966 the first manuscript was finished, published in 1968 by the Hoover Institution at Stanford University as *Western Technology And Soviet Economic Development 1917 to 1930*. After 1968, the research moved more quickly. In 1970, Volume Two was published with the same title covering the years 1930 to 1945 — the years of the famous Five Year Plans, which, by the way, were completely of Western construction and origin. Volume Three (1945 to 1965) was completed in mid-1970 but delayed in press for three and one-half years, for political reasons, and not made available to the public until early 1974. Recently, this writer's *National Suicide: Military Aid To The Soviet Union* was published. This is a first attempt to probe our long-run and continuing military assistance to the Soviet Union.*

National Suicide was originally published in 1973. The author is currently working on a revised and expanded version of this work, to be published in 1978 by '76 Press under the title, *Wall Street and Soviet Military Power*.

Each of these four volumes has the same methodology. Major processes and equipment in use in the U.S.S.R. are examined to trace the design origins. In the steel industry, for example, Soviet adoption of the classical blast furnace for production of pig iron is examined, as well as electric furnaces, open-hearth furnaces, hot and cold wide-strip mills, pipe mills, and so on. In each case, the adoption and history of the process used inside the Soviet Union is detailed. Steam locomotives, electric locomotives, truck engines, chemical processes, and so on — the whole range of modern industrial production technology — are similarly described.

Let's take one industrial sector, the Soviet merchant marine, in more detail. This will illustrate the methodology, and the amount of verifiable technical detail it has been possible to acquire, and the overall conclusions. The merchant marine is chosen because a ship has a simple well-known technology (hull plus engine), and the conclusions can be easily verified in any major library.

The Soviet merchant marine has about 6,000 ships listed in the Soviet Register of Shipping. This Register has a great amount of accurate technical detail: dimensions/weight/engine specifications, right down to cylinder diameter, piston stroke, and type of diesel or other propulsion system used.

In 1930, the Soviet fleet carried only about 4 percent of Russian-generated cargo, and up to the 1950s the Soviet merchant marine was very small. In the early 1950s a massive construction and acquisition program of merchant ships was begun. The Soviet Union now has the most modern merchant marine in the world, and among the largest in numbers and tonnage.

The analysis of this Soviet merchant marine examined two criteria: (a) the origin of the ship hulls in these Soviet ships; and, (b) the origin of their propulsion systems.

Each of the 6,000 entries in the Soviet shipping register, which has more information than Lloyds Register, was examined, and two statistics calculated: (1) how many hulls in these ships were built *inside* the U.S.S.R.; (2) how many hulls were built *outside* the U.S.S.R. Then it was calculated: (1) how many engines in these ships were built *inside* the U.S.S.R.; (2) how many engines were built *outside* the U.S.S.R.

This method is precise. It is accurate. Unless there is a mistake in arithmetic, the figures cannot be challenged. No one has yet.

The results of this statistical analysis are extraordinary. When we break down the Soviet data — and it is emphasized that this is *Soviet* data — we find that from 1918 to 1968: (1) 34 percent (only about one-third) of Soviet merchant ship hulls were built *inside* the U.S.S.R.; and, (2) 80 percent (four-fifths) of Soviet merchant ship diesel engines were built *outside* the U.S.S.R.

But even the one-fifth of "Soviet" marine diesel engines built *inside* the U.S.S.R. was built with foreign technical assistance, either Skoda or Burmeister & Wain design, and manufactured with technical assistance from these firms. *In brief, there is no such thing as a purely Soviet-designed marine diesel engine, and never has been.*

In themselves, these are interesting statistics for economists, and radically different from the contemporary textbook image of Soviet economic development. But when we view these same statistics in the context of national security, they become of critical importance, and it is obvious why the proponents of political *détente* refuse even to consider this evidence. The statistics reveal *détente* not only to be an illusion but also a first-rate danger to the survival of the West. Promoters of *détente* argue, for example, that "merchant ships are peaceful goods," and "we can sell merchant ships to the Soviet Union and this will not affect our national defense."

How true is this statement?

A list of the 96 Soviet ships used to supply North Vietnam through the port of Haiphong was analyzed. Out of the 96 ships, 84 were identified, the other 12 ships were of too recent construction to be listed in the Soviet Shipping Register. All of these 84 identifiable ships except 13 (*i.e.*, 71 out of the 84) were built *outside* the U.S.S.R. The 13 exceptions were diesel ships built *inside* the U.S.S.R. with engines to Skoda or Burmeister & Wain specifications and with their technical assistance.

In other words, none of the identifiable Soviet supply ships on the Haiphong run — supplying the Vietnam War — had a Soviet-designed propulsion system. Almost all the marine propulsion units in these ships (71 out of 84 were identified) were built *outside* the U.S.S.R., and all were designed *outside* the U.S.S.R.

Even more significant: The faster and larger Soviet ships were built in the West. The Western-built ships on the Haiphong supply run were about 20 percent faster than Soviet-built ships. This is not guesswork, it is a precise calculation.

Logically, then, the Soviets could not have supplied North Vietnam (and they provided about 80 percent of the weapons and supplies) without this prior Western technical assistance and construction of merchant ships. One cannot argue that the Soviets would have substituted "Soviet" ships. The Soviet-built component is only 34 percent of the hulls and zero percent of the marine diesel designs.

Consequently, the 100,000 Americans and countless allies killed in Korea and Vietnam were killed with armaments transported on propulsion systems we ourselves supplied. This is a logical, inescapable conclusion. You cannot avoid it. It is a fact, and obviously a highly important fact for national security.

Vietnam and Cambodia are now lost to the West. They are lost because we in the West supplied the material means to wage the war on the other side. We can arrive at these conclusions not only for the merchant marine, but for most other Soviet industrial sectors *including the inputs for weapons technology*.

There is a fundamental problem of analysis, which explains in part why this evidence and the conclusions have not been understood, nor even recognized, by Western governments. The methodology we have used in the past to discuss Soviet trade is faulty.

There is *the Problem of the Margin*: Economic theory has a rule which states that *the Sum of the Margins equals the Total*. The problem in our analysis of Soviet trade is that businessmen, government officials, and defense analysts have been looking at the *Margin* instead of the *Total*. Looking at the Total leads to different answers and completely different conclusions.

A shipbuilder sells *one* merchant ship to the Soviets. In economics this is called the marginal unit, the last unit sold. The shipbuilder goes to his government export control office and says "we only want to sell *one* merchant ship, can we have an export permit for this?" The sale cannot affect national security, it is only a single ship, and one ship makes an insignificant contribution to Soviet capability. The export control officials say, "O.K. It's only one ship and that will not hurt national security." So the shipbuilder gets an order and a permit for the one ship, and the Soviets ultimately add it to their merchant marine.

Then the next shipbuilder comes along and makes the same argument. And so on. Each seller, each businessman, each government official, looks at the *one* unit, the marginal unit, or the last unit sold.

The research outlined above sums *all* the units sold from 1917 to 1970 — the total. In other words, the sum of the marginal units. When you look at the total picture you come up with completely different answers. In the last half-dozen years we have — under so-called *détente* — brought the Soviet Union to a substantially new technological level and created extraordinary strategic disadvantages that the West will have to face in coming years. The Soviets didn't do this, we did it — or rather Henry Kissinger and the multinationals did it. In six words: *We have built ourselves an enemy*.

Now a businessman is not at all concerned with national defense; he is interested only in the sale under negotiation. His interest is in selling a plant today. A businessman doesn't care what was sold in 1926 or 1956, or what will be sold in 1986. The government official should care, but he is subject to political influences, and no U.S. Government official is going to fight Henry Kissinger.

So when I.C.I. sells a chemical plant to the Soviet Union, I.C.I. concerns itself only with the single sale, not the total Russian chemical industry. When Boeing Aircraft sells aircraft technology to the U.S.S.R., it considers only a single aircraft or a single process — for example, the door technology for the Boeing 707 — not all Russian technology. When Fiat sells an auto plant to the U.S.S.R., it concerns itself only with that one auto plant, not all Soviet auto plants.

Business and government are concerned with single sales, whereas realistic analysis should concern the total picture of single sales over 50 years. When you examine this total picture it is obvious that we in effect create not only our own strategic and defense problems, but also provide a motivation for revolutionaries and subversives to *be* revolutionaries and subversives.

What can we project for our security on the basis of these research findings, using this concept of total transfers over 50 years rather than individual sales or short-term programs such as Henry Kissinger's *détente?* Some fairly definite statements and projections can be made.

First, so long as the Soviet Union and Red China retain their planned economic systems, with political and ideological manipulation of economic decisions, neither country will attain significant self-generated technological development. Both countries will remain the technical captives of the West. A planned society is also a static society. A planned society is not a technologically viable society; that is, it cannot progress technologically. But a planned society can still go to war. It can still be a breeding ground for revolutionaries. That is what we must keep in mind.

Second, both Russia and Red China have been able to present a universally accepted image of vigorous and viable socialist societies because of our continuous injections of Western technology. They are technologically viable only because we make them so. This technical subsidy has enabled Communists to undertake two fundamental policies: (a) to continue worldwide expansion; (b) to provide an ideological objective for terrorists and subversives who want to convert the Western societies into what they see as progressive socialist societies.

The Far Left in Portugal has as an objective a planned Marxist society. But these Portuguese Marxists, the terrorists in Africa and domestic subversives, *would have no cause to fight for if we allowed Russia and China to reveal to the world their inherent economic and technical deficiencies.* No self-respecting revolutionary is going to fight for an inefficient backward system. Most revolutionaries visualize a glorious picture-book society with bread for all, perhaps a piece of land or an automobile, not a backward stagnant society. Therefore, *we* suffer revolution and subversion in our world because *we* provide a rationale and an objective for revolutionaries through our subsidy of inefficient and ineffective socialist systems.

The most important supporters of socialism are those Western businessmen who give credibility to the Soviet system through technical transfers. These are the same businessmen who indirectly provide an image of credibility for socialist systems and so give birth to revolutionaries. In brief the revolutionaries and subverters exist only through the support of our own businessmen, and it is ironic that some of these same businessmen are often in the forefront of demanding action against the same revolutionaries and subverters they have themselves created.

So as we continue to subsidize Communist countries under the theory of *détente*, we shall see more terrorism, not less. *More* subversion, not less. More Portugals and more Allendes. In the long run we create our own problems. If we want to halt revolution, terrorism, and Communist expansion, the key is in the hands of Western businessmen. All they have to do is turn the key in the lock and shut off the technical subsidy. In the final analysis it is that simple.

They will not do it. Why not?

Western businessmen fall over themselves to demonstrate they are in business because they have a "social conscience" which has priority over profits. Yet these same businessmen will not turn a hair at supplying the technology that kills their allies (and workers) by the millions.

There is a major credibility gap among many anti-Communists. Some anti-Communists have long recognized that we create our own problems. Other anti-Communists, including businessmen trading with the U.S.S.R., refuse to recognize the facts or the problem. This schism among anti-Communists is now obvious, and is developing as far away as Australia, New Zealand, and Latin America, although it has long been identifiable in the United States. In the U.S. one can freely discuss Communism and Communist revolution up to a point — and *only* up to the point — where one identifies those who subsidize revolution and make possible the long-run survival of socialist ideas and systems.

Therefore, because of the nature of the total picture of our technical subsidy of Communism, we now have to go beyond the subverters and the revolutionaries and look at the actions and motivations of the subsidizers — those who make possible and encourage the actions of the subverters and revolutionaries. That is going to be the core test of the credibility of Free Enterprise arguments in the coming years.

When we discuss the subsidy of socialist systems we separate those who truly want our Western society to survive from those who are playing semantic games with our survival or gambling with our survival for personal profit.

Further, the current cliché about convergence among political systems for a New World Order is suspect. Convergence will mean a static socialist world. As we subsidize the socialist world, we are at the same time undermining our own world of Free Enterprise. Convergence is not some half-way point, convergence is a socialized world with no individual freedom and no enterprise opportunities.

Finally, these problems cannot be considered in a vacuum. On the one hand we have subsidized the economic and military power of the Soviet Union. We donate viability to a static failure-prone economic system. We provide the rationale and motivation for revolution and subversion. However, there is another facet to this problem: rampant, uncontrollable inflation resulting from an ostensible attempt to achieve full employment; our own quasi-socialist planning which more obviously reveals the defects of socialism. We are on the edge of a financial precipice which will bring down the financial structure of the Western world. Or, to change the metaphor, our big balloon of debt and fiat money is poised to come crashing down on our heads. When it does ("when," not "if"), we can expect social and economic chaos. This chaos will make our Western society an easy victim for the Marxists, the revolutionaries, the subversives, and their friends.

In considering our future survival, two interrelated elements can be identified: (1) the technical and financial subsidy of the Soviet Union which provides an unworkable and hostile system with the illusion of success, and so encourages the revolutionaries and subversives; and, (2) an on-going crisis of a collapsing world financial system which ultimately will create chaos, an essential prerequisite for successful revolution and the overthrow of capitalist society.

If we assume that businessmen wish to live in a Free Enterprise system, that they cherish their country and its enterprise traditions, then two basic policies have to be adopted. These are fundamentally new policies. The trend of the last 50 years has brought us to the brink of disaster, and new policies are wholly opposed to, and inconsistent with, this trend. They are wholly opposed to the Kissinger-Rockefeller approach.

Briefly, it is recommended that we must undertake these policies:

(1) To neutralize the widespread illusion that socialist societies have any technical and economic viability, that socialism can in any way be successful without our help. This is an educational task. It cannot be done by legislation or by government decree. The task has to be undertaken by private organizations and private individuals.

(2) To adopt a world financial system based on the ultimate discipline of gold. Preferably a pure gold standard, but any international system based on gold would restore confidence in currency. This is a political task.

If industry adopts and implements these policies reasonably soon, it is still possible for Free Enterprise to survive and prosper. If industry does not adopt these policies, then a bleak future faces the Western world. We shall see either a world Communist state, or more probably a world community of Communist states, within several decades. Probably by the year 2000, perhaps sooner, not much later.

So there is still a little time. But not too much time.

APPENDIX C

HARD MONEY ORGANIZATIONS, INVESTMENT ADVISERS AND MARKET NEWSLETTERS

There are several active organizations devoted to hard-money education which publish books, pamphlets and newsletters reporting current events. The following list is not exhaustive, by any means.

NATIONAL COMMITTEE FOR MONETARY REFORM (formerly the National Committee to Legalize Gold). Address: 1524 Hillary Street, New Orleans, Louisiana 70118 (Telephone: 504 865-9919). National Director: James U. Blanchard III. This Committee publishes *Gold Newsletter* ($20.00 per year) and was probably the most influential single lobbying factor is gaining legalization of gold ownership for American citizens. The Committee holds well-attended, informative conferences each year.

COMMITTEE FOR MONETARY RESEARCH. Address: P.O. Box 1630. Greenwich, Connecticut 06830 (Telephone: 203 661-2533). Secretary: Elizabeth Bricker Currier. Publishes a series of Monetary Tracts (see Selected Bibliography), holds annual Arden House conferences on monetary reform. It is more academically oriented than N.C.M.R.

AMERICAN INSTITUTE FOR ECONOMIC RESEARCH. Address: Great Barrington, Massachusetts 01230. This is Colonel Harwood's Institute. It has specialized in research and publication in the field of sound money for many decades. Any reader who has doubts about the accuracy of the forecasts made in the government and academic world will enjoy the AIER report, "Useless Economic Forecasting" (March 22, 1976).

SOME MARKET ADVISORY AND NEWSLETTERS:*

Donald J. Hoppe Business and Investment Analysis,
Box 513, Crystal Lake, Illinois 60014 ($100.00 per year).
Baxter Economic Service,
1030 E. Putnam Avenue, Greenwich, Connecticut 06830 ($108.00 per year).
Deak-Perera Digest,
29 Broadway, New York, New York 10006 ($100.00 per year).
Dow Theory Letters,
P.O. Box 1759, La Jolla, California 92038 ($125.00 per year).
Daily News Digest,
P.O. Box 27496, Phoenix, Arizona 85061 ($90.00 per year).
The Forecaster,
19623 Ventura Boulevard, Tarzana, California 91356 ($90.00 per year).
Heim Investment Letter,
812 S.W. Washington Street, Suite 600, Portland, Oregon 97205 ($150.00 per year).
The Holt Investment Advisory,
277 Park Avenue, New York, New York 10017 ($144.00 per year).
Gold,
P.O. Box 2523, Lausanne 1002, Switzerland ($150.00 per year).
Silver and Gold Report,
P.O. Box 472, Norwalk, Connecticut 06856 ($144.00 per year).
Remnant Review,
P.O. Box 1580, Springfield, Virginia 22151.
Metals and Monetary Report,
1511 K Street N.W., Washington, D.C. 20005 ($45.00 per year).
McShane Letter,
155 East 55th Street, New York, New York 10022 ($80.00 per year).
The Macaskill Letter,
P.O. Box 576, Florida 1710, Republic of South Africa ($115.00 per year).

---

*For a complete listing, send $1.00 to the National Committee for Monetary Reform in New Orleans.

North American Client Advisory,
100 West Washington Street, Phoenix, Arizona 85003.
International Gold Reports,
Alert Buildings, De La Warr Road, Bexhill on Sea, Sussex, England.
International Moneyline,
21 Charles Street, Westport, Connecticut 06880 ($15.00 per month).
L. T. Patterson Strategy Letter,
Postfach 987, 4001 Basel, Switzerland ($75.00 per year).
International Harry Schultz Letter,
P.O. Box 2523, Lausanne 1002, Switzerland ($225.00 per year).
National Coin Reporter Hard Asset and Currency Review,
P.O. Box 7212, Chicago, Illinois 60680 ($4.00 per issue).
Value-Action Advisory Service,
3838 48th Avenue N.E., Seattle, Washington 98105.
The Bank Credit Analyst,
Butterfield Building, Front Street, Hamilton, Bermuda ($275.00 per year).
Viewpoints,
Institute for Monetary Research, Inc., 1010 Vermont Avenue, N.W., Washington, D.C. 20005

SELECTED BIBLIOGRAPHY

Allen, Gary. *None Dare Call It Conspiracy*. Seal Beach, California: Concord Press, 1972.

American Institute for Economic Research. *Is There an Upper Limit to the Price of Gold?* December, 1973.

_____. *The "New" International Monetary System*, Part IV IMF Agreements. Massachusetts, February 2, 1976.

_____. Economic Research Economic Education Bulletin, Volume XII, Number 12, *Paper Gold*. Edited by Ernest Welker. Massachusetts, December, 1972.

Aron, J. *Annual Review and Outlook*. New York: Aron and Company, Inc., January, 1976.

_____. *Gold Statistics and Analysis*, October, 1975. New York: J. Aron and Company, Inc., 1975.

Bailey, Norman A. *Brazil as a Monetary Model*, Monetary Tract, Number 10. Connecticut: Committee for Monetary Research and Education, Inc., June, 1975.

Bakewell, Paul Jr. *Inflation in the United States*. Idaho: The Caxton Printers, Ltd., 1962.

Berger, Rene. *The Failure of International Monetary Cooperation*, Monetary Tract, Number 1. Connecticut: Committee for Monetary Research and Education, Inc., November, 1973.

Boarman, Patrick M. *Floating Exchange Rates and World-Wide Inflation*, Monetary Tract, Number 13. Connecticut: Committee for Monetary Research and Education, Inc., February, 1976.

Brahmananda, P. R. *The Gold-Money Rift*. Bombay: Popular Brakashan, n.d.

Bresciani-Turroni, Constantino. *The Economics of Inflation*. New York: Kelly, 1968.

Brown, Robert S. *Monetary Mismanagement and the Role of Gold*, Monetary Tract, Number 14. Connecticut: Committee for Monetary Research and Education, Inc., April, 1976.

Burns, A. R. *Money and Monetary Policy in Early Times*. London: Kegan Paul, Trench Trubner and Company, Ltd., 1927.

Busschau, W. J. *Gold and International Liquidity, The Flow of Credit in Relation to Gold in the International Monetary System*. Johannesburg, South Africa: The South African Institute of International Affairs, 1961.

Cannan, Edwin. *The Paper Pound of 1797-1821*. London: P. S. King and Son, Ltd., 1919.

Carroll, Charles Holt. *Organization of Debt into Currency and Other Papers*. New Jersey: D. Van Nostrand Company, Inc., 1964.

Cobbett, William. *Paper Against Gold*. London: William Cobbett, 1828.

Consolidated Gold Fields Limited. *The Chairman's Review for 1975*. London: 1975.

_____. *Gold 1975*. London: June, 1975.

Del Mar, Alexander. *The History of Money in America*. Reprint, Hawthorne: Omni, 1966.

Dines, James. *The Invisible Crash*. New York: Random House, 1975.

Federal Reserve System. *The Federal Reserve System: Purposes and Functions*. Washington, D.C.: Federal Reserve System.

Fisher, Irving. *100% Money*. New York: Adelphi Company, 1935.

Forbes, William. *The Memoirs of a Banking House*. Edinburgh, Scotland: privately published, 1859.

Friedman, Milton and Schwartz, Anna Jacobson. *A Monetary History of the United State, 1857-1960*. Princeton: Princeton University Press, 1963.

Gire, David E. *Social Security: You Pay More - But Will You Get More?* Monetary Tract, Number 12. Connecticut: Committee for Monetary Research and Education, Inc., January, 1976.

Gold in South Africa. South Africa: Chamber of Mines of South Africa, n.d.

Gouge, William M. *A Short History of Paper Money and Banking in the United State*. New York: Augustus M. Kelley Publishers, 1968.

Greaves, Percy L., Jr. *Understanding the Dollar Crisis*. Boston: Western Islands, 1973.

Green, Timothy, *The World of Gold Today*. New York: Walker and Company, 1973.

Hazlitt, Henry. *The Failure of the New Economics*. New York: Arlington House, 1959.

Hillendahl, Wesley H. *Big Government's Destruction of the American Economy*. Monetary Tract, Number 4. Connecticut: Committee for Monetary Research and Education, Inc., July, 1964.

Holloway, John E. *Inflation and Un-Earned Money*, Monetary Tract, Number 9. Connecticut: Committee for Monetary Research and Education, Inc., April, 1975.

International Monetary Fund. *International Financial Statistics*, Volume XXVIII, Number 12. Washington: 1975.

_____. *International Monetary Reform*, Documents of the Committee of Twenty. Washington, D.C.: 1974.

_____. *Proposed Second Amendment to the Articles of Agreement of the International Monetary Fund*, A Report by the Executive Directors to the Board of Governors. Washington: International Monetary Fund, March, 1976.

_____. *Selected Decisions of the International Monetary Fund and Selected Documents, Seventh Issue.* Washington, D.C.: January 1, 1975.

_____. *Summary Proceedings Annual Meeting 1974.* September 30-October 4, 1974. Washington D.C.

Investors' Press. *The Gold Boom of the 70s*, Commentary and Forecasts on Gold and Gold Shares 1969-1974. New Jersey: 1974.

Kemmerer, Donald L. *The Gold Standard and Economic Growth*, Monetary Tract, Number 6. Connecticut: Committee for Monetary Research and Education, Inc., October, 1974.

Kemp, Arthur. *The Legal Qualities of Money.* New York: Pageant Press, 1956.

Kenan, H. S. *The Federal Reserve Bank.* Los Angeles: Noontide Press, 1966.

Keynes, John Maynard. *The General Theory of Employment Interest and Money.* New York: Harcourt, Brace and Company, n.d.

_____. *A Treatise on Money, Volume 1, The Pure Theory of Money.* London: Macmillan & Company, Ltd., 1958.

_____. *A Treatise on Money, Volume II, The Applied Theory of Money.* London: Macmillan & Compaay, Ltd., 1960.

Kriz, Miroslav. *Washington and the Future of Gold*, Monetary Tract, Number 3. Connecticut: Committee for Monetary Research and Education, Inc., May, 1974.

Laursen, Karsten and Pedersen, Jorgen. *The German Inflation, 1918-1923.* Amsterdam: North Holland Publishing Company, 1964.

Leiss, Amelie Co. *Apartheid and United Nations Collective Measures.* New York: Carnegie Endowment for International Peace, 1965.

Littlepage, John D. *In Search of Soviet Gold.* London: George G. Harrap, 1939.

Marker, Richard A. *The IMF - Engine of Inflation, The Future of Currencies and Gold and How You Can Survive and Profit.* California: Forecaster Publishing Company, 1975.

McLaughlin, Donald H. *The Triumph of Gold*, Monetary Tract, Number 2. Connecticut: Committee for Monetary Research and Education, Inc., February, 1974.

von Mises, Ludwig. *Human Action - A Treatise on Economics*. London: William Hodges and Company Ltd., 1949.

_____. *The Theory of Money and Credit*. New York: The Foundation for Economic Education, Inc., 1971.

Mullins, Eustace. *The Federal Reserve Conspiracy*. New Jersey: Christian Educational Association, 1954.

Nugent, Walter T. K. *Money and American Society 1865-1880*. New York: The Free Press, 1968.

Oudard, Georges. *The Amazing Life of John Law*. New York: Payson & Clarke, 1928.

Palyi, Melchior, *The Twilight of Gold, 1914-1936*. Chicago: Henry Regnery Company, 1972.

Paris, Alexander P. *The Coming Credit Collapse*. New York: Arlington House Publishers, 1974.

Pick, Franz. *1975 Pick's Currency Yearbook*. New York: 21 West Street, 10006, 1975.

Rees-Mogg, William. *The Reigning Error*. London: Hamilton Publishers, 1974.

Rickenbacker, William F. *Death of the Dollar*. New York: Dell Publishing Company, Inc., 1968.

Ridgeway, William. *The Origin of Coin and Weight Standards*. Cambridge: 1892.

Ringer, Fritz K. *The German Inflation of 1923*. London/New York: Oxford University Press, 1969.

Robbins, John W. *The Case Against Indexation*, Monetary Tract, Number 16. Connecticut: Committee for Monetary Research and Education, Inc., July 1976.

Royal Institute of International Affairs. *The International Gold Problem*. London: Oxford Press, 1931.

Rueff, Jacques. *Balance of Payments*. New York: The Macmillan Company, 1967.

_____. *The Monetary Sin of the West*. New York: The Macmillan Company, 1972.

_____. *The Worldwide Inflation and Its Causes*, Monetary Tract, Number 8. Connecticut: Committee for Monetary Research and Education, Inc., March, 1975.

Salter, F. R. *Sir Thomas Gresham 1518-1579*. London: Leonard Parsona and Boston: Small, Maynard and Company, n.d.

Schloss, Henry H. *The Bank for International Settlements*. Amsterdam: North-Holland Publishing Company, 1958.

Sennholz, Hans, F. *Gold is Money*, Contributions in Economic History, Number 12. Westport, Connecticut: Greenwood Press, 1975.

Smith, Adam. *Supermoney*. New York: Popular Library, 1975.

Snyder, Leslie. *Gold and Black Gold*. New York: Exposition Press, 1974.

Spahr, Walter E. *Our Irredeemable Currency System*, Monetary Tract, Number 15. Connecticut: Committee for Monetary Research and Education, Inc., June, 1976.

Sumner, William Graham. *The Financier and the Finances of the French Revolution*. New York: Dodd, Mead, 1892.

Sutton, Antony C. *National Suicide: Military Aid to the Soviet Union*. New York: Arlington House, 1973.

_____. *Wall Street and the Bolshevik Revolution*. New York: Arlington House, 1974.

Thornton, Henry, *An Enquiry Into the Nature and Effects of the Paper Credit of Great Britain, 1802*. New York: Farrar & Rinehart, Inc., 1939.

Triffin, Robert. *Europe and the Money Muddle*. New Haven: Yale University Press, 1957.

_____. *Gold and the Dollar Crisis*, The Future of Convertibility. New Haven: Yale University Press, 1960.

Unger, Irwin. *The Greenback Era*. New Jersey: Princeton University Press, 1964.

U.S. House. *Implementation of the U.S. Arms Embargo*. Hearing before the Subcommittee on Africa of the Committee on Foreign Affairs. Washington: 1973.

_____. Report of the Subcommittee on International Trade, Investment and Monetary Policy of the Committee on Banking, Currency and Housing. *Exchange Rate Policy and International Monetary Reform*. 94th Congress, First Session. Washington: August, 1975.

_____. Hearings before the Subcommittee on International Trade, Investment and Monetary Policy of the Committee on Banking, Currency and Housing. *International Monetary Reform and Exchange Rate Management*. 94th Congress, First Session. Washington: July 17, 18, 21, 1975.

_____. Report of the Subcommittee on International Economics of the Joint Economic Committee, *The Proposed IMF Agreement on Gold*. Washington: 1975.

Vissering, W. *On Chinese Currency, Coin and Paper Money*. Taipei: Ch'Eng Wen Publishing Company, 1968.

Webster, Pelatiah. *Not Worth A Continental*. New York: The Foundation for Economic Education, 1950.

White, Andrew Dickson. *Fiat Money Inflation in France*. Toronto: Canada, privately published, 1914.

Wiegand, G. C., Editor. *Inflation and Monetary Crisis*, A Symposium of the Committee for Monetary Research and Education. Washington, D.C.: Public Affairs Press, 1975.

_____. *Toward a New World Monetary System*, Proceedings at First Arden House International Monetary Conference. New York: McGraw-Hill, n.d.

Wormser, Rene A. and Hemmerer, Donald L., *Restoring "Gold Clauses" in Contracts*, Monetary Tract, Number 7. Connecticut: Committee for Monetary Research and Education, Inc., January, 1975.

INDEX

A

Aldrich, Nelson - 84

American Bankers Assn. - 160

American City National Bank and Trust Co. - 137

American Institute Counselors - 124-126

American Institute for Economic Research - 124-126

Angola - 194, 195, 206

Apartheid and United Nations Collective Measures - 192

assignats - 32, 34, 36-37, 41, 68, 108

Argentina - 72, 135, 143

Aristophanes - 121

A Short History of Banking & Paper Money in the United States - 31, 51

B

balance of payments - 100-101, 110, 135, 157, 183

Bank for International Settlements - 75, 147, 154-156, 163, 165, 171

Bank of England - 36, 37, 39, 40, 42, 43, 116, 152

Bank of Chidester of Arkansas - 137

Bank of Scotland - 37, 38

Bank Restriction Act of 1797 - 41

Bantu - 191

Baring, Alexander - 41

Barrons - 112

barter - 27

Belgium - 111, 119, 152

Bennett, Jack F. - 113, 157

Bermudez, Morales - 195

Beverly Hills Bancorp - 137

Beverly Hills National Bank - 137

bezant - 23, 24, 27

Bilderburgers - 193

Black Muslims - 169

Botswama - 149

Bretton Woods Agreement - 100, 146-148, 150, 154

Brezhnev, Leonid - 169

Britain - *see*, England

Bryon, William Jennings - 51, 55

Bullion Committee (Britain) - 41-43, 161

Bullion Report of 1810 - 41-44

Bureau of the Mint - 114, 115

Burns, A. R. - 20, 27

Burns, Arthur - 127, 141

Business Week - 60

Byzantine Empire - 19, 27, 200

C

California, gold coins minted - 55

Calvin, O. Walter - 91

Canute, King - 48, 110

Carli, Guido - 112, 173

Carnegie Endowment for International Peace - 192, 194, 196, 207

Carter, Jimmy - 63

Central Intelligence Agency - 195

Chamberlain, John - 99

Chase Manhattan Bank - 85, 132, 135, 138-139

Chase Manhattan Mortgage & Realty - 132

Chatham House Study Group - 69

Chemical Bank of New York - 137

chervonetz - 64, 168